The Wisdom of Life Through My Patients

The
Wisdom of Life
Through My Patients

Thomas P. Waldinger, M.D.

Dearborn, Michigan, 1999

A portion of the proceeds from this book will be donated to the
University of Michigan Comprehensive Cancer Center,
Ann Arbor, Michigan, in honor of
John L. Ulrich, M.D.

Produced by csw designs, inc.

ISBN 0-9672436-0-2

Editor: Bette Mys
Designer: Carol S. Wyatt

Printed in the United States of America
First Edition

2002 2001 2000 1999   5 4 3 2

In Loving Memory

John L. Ulrich, M. D.

To my great mentor and friend
Your wisdom guided me
Your warmth and kindness lifted me
Your medical tradition continues.

and

A.M. Powell

The grandfather who loved me
The time was too short
You are with me now
Your legacy continues.

Always on My Shoulder

You showed me the way
From dust to breath
From dawn to dusk
You showed me the way.

If I had wings
I would fly
Rest on the clouds
Search every star.

To tell you
Deep in my heart
You will always be
You showed me the way
Always on my shoulder.

Renewal of spring
Warmth of summer
Color of autumn
Snow of winter is falling
The symphony of seasons
Always on my shoulder.

Leaves appear on the trees
Swans settle on the lake
Lake Run Rainbow swim upstream
Swallows fly south
The symphony of seasons
Always on my shoulder.

So this is where I am
Settled in my soul
Every day I remember
Memories are forever.

If I had wings
I would fly
Rest on the clouds
Search every star.

To tell you
Deep in my heart
You will always be
You showed me the way
Always on my shoulder.

T.P.W.

Contents

Acknowledgments

To my wife, Marcy, who with her love and support made my dream become a reality. I feel the same way today as the first moment I saw you.

To Jason and Emily with love.

> "The day
> you were born,
> somewhere a flower
> bloomed, the sun shone
> even brighter, and
> when the wind
> moved over the
> ocean, it whispered
> your name. . ."

> – Lynne Gerard

To Mrs. John Ulrich, the wife of my special friend and mentor. Thank you for always treating me in such a kind, caring and thoughtful manner. You are very special to my family and me. May God bless you.

To Bette and Don Mys, whose support, enthusiasm and keen intellect have been invaluable. In the process of seeking your wisdom, a lifetime friendship was formed. Your belief in me and the book created a synergy that allowed me to reach a greater height.

To Jan Smith for your assistance with so many aspects of the book. Nothing was too much for you to undertake and your persistence and commitment to this project are sincerely appreciated. You were always willing to help in any way. I am confident that the book would never have been a reality without you, Jan. Thank you so much for everything.

To Mary Sharon Joseph for your enormous help with the editing of this publication. Your gentle counsel and journalistic talent enabled me to successfully complete the book. You embraced my work and were always there to guide me.

To Alice Nigoghosian, Associate Director, Wayne State University Press. Thank you so much for sharing your encouragement, interest, experience and intellect throughout every aspect of the book. Your willingness to share your thoughts and ideas in the midst of an extremely busy schedule will always be appreciated.

To Carol Wyatt. Your outstanding expertise, positive energy and friendship were much appreciated in the preparation of this publication.

To my current medical staff. You not only helped with the care of my patients, but also provided invaluable assistance with several aspects of this book:

Mrs. Pansy Combs, Mrs. Lois Ragsdale, Ms. Jaime Sutherland, Mrs. Kathy Becker, Mrs. Andi Goward, Ms. Leslee Litrich, Mrs. Beverly Miller, Mrs. Jan Smith, Mrs. Debbie Taft, Ms. Nicole Woodruff, Ms. Danielle Bzovi, Mrs. Joanne Beasley, and Ms. Jennifer McCart.

To my previous staff members. Your efforts on behalf of Dr. Ulrich and me are remembered each day:

Mrs. Phyllis Preston, Ms. Bertha Denhard, Mrs. Shirley Smith, Mrs. Ernestine Maycock, Mrs. Eleanore Tauriainen, Mrs. Daisy McCune, Mrs. Verlene Wells, Mrs. Joan Sall, Mrs. Sharon Martin, Mrs. Marcia Wheeler, Mrs. Sherry Fuhrman, Ms. Linda Edwards, Mrs. Christine Russell, Ms. Elaine Chrapkiewicz, Mrs. Sherry Ossy, Ms. Lisa Rusnak, and Mrs. Brenda Hannah-Bergman.

I would also like to recognize the contributions, interest and support from the following patients and friends:

William G. Abbatt, Esquire; Ms. Susan Corney; Mr. Carley Tolliver; Bernard Reilly, A.D.; Mr. Steve Ford; Mrs. Betty Szekely; Mr. Duane Black; and Ms. E. Jane Noxon.

To Colin Day, Director; Rebecca McDermott, Editor for Health Policy and Management; and Michael Kehoe, Marketing Director, of the University of Michigan Press. Thank you for your interest, commitment to excellence, and professionalism. It is gratifying for me to once again establish ties with the University of Michigan.

To all my cherished patients. You have given me so much. You are an inspiration to me each day.

To my parents. Thank you for your love and support. You are always in my prayers.

Foreword

A chance of a lifetime,
What is life?

Life is a gift. . .accept.
Life is an adventure. . .dare it.
Life is a mystery. . .unfold it.
Life is struggle. . .face it.
Life is beauty. . .praise it.
Life is a puzzle. . .solve it.
Life is opportunity. . .take it.
Life is sorrowful. . .experience it.
Life is a song. . .sing it.
Life is a goal. . .achieve it.
Life is a mission. . .fulfill it.
Our life has a purpose. . .find it.

Thoughts for a lifetime.

Bette Mys, Editor

Introduction

This book is written to honor the memory of John L. Ulrich,
M.D. Dr. Ulrich had the most profound effect on my adult
and professional life.

In 1984, I was completing the final year of my dermatology
residency at the University of Michigan Medical Center and
interviewing across the country to determine where to establish
my practice. I was interested in potential practices in Wisconsin
and Florida when I learned that a dermatologist in Dearborn,
Michigan, was seeking an associate.

I had the opportunity to meet Dr. Ulrich at his office the third
Saturday in October 1984. I felt a tremendous warmth, caring
and spiritual quality from him. I remember his smile and pleasant voice. Dr. Ulrich proceeded to give me a tour through the
office and then we sat in an examination room to talk. I couldn't
help but notice that the mural in this exam room–a country
scene with a meadow, pond, trees and a waterwheel–was the
same wallpaper as in the dining room of my home. At the end of
our first meeting, Dr. Ulrich looked at me in his warm, compassionate way and said, "God bless you and your family." As I sat
with Dr. Ulrich, I knew that this was the person I wanted to join
in practice.

There was only one other defining moment in my life. In 1974, my sophomore year of college, while studying in the dormitory library and absorbed in a chemistry book, I looked up across the room and noticed a friend of mine coming to say hello. She was accompanied by a woman I had never seen before. I immediately knew, even before we were introduced, that this was the person I wanted to marry. This was particularly striking because marriage was the furthest thing from my mind and I was concentrating on my pre-medical studies. Our mutual friend introduced Marcy to me that day in the library. We were married in 1977 and this past June celebrated our 21st anniversary.

These two events changed the course of my life.

On July 1, 1985, I began practicing dermatology with Dr. Ulrich. I noticed that Dr. Ulrich had a most remarkable connection with each of his patients. The first day at lunch, he told me that it was very important to have a genuine love and concern for each patient. He also said that if you truly love and care for your patients and do everything medically possible that you can, God will take care of the rest. Although Dr. Ulrich was 40 years my senior and from a different era, I had truly met my kindred spirit because we shared the same philosophy. We worked together on Mondays and Wednesdays for five years, sharing a small office with only three exam rooms. We always brought lunch from home and ate together in our office.

I vividly remember that upon leaving in the evening, Dr. Ulrich would always say, "God bless you." He always shared the same special warmth and caring with me that he extended to his patients. He was so sincere that this had great meaning for me. I was able to talk to him about all of my concerns. He would listen carefully, offer his advice, but always emphasize "to give it to the Lord." During my first several months of practice, Dr. Ulrich would not accept payment for his services because he said I needed "time to get on my feet." This is another example of the generosity and thoughtfulness of this very special human being.

On the Saturday of Labor Day weekend, several weeks before Dr. Ulrich passed away, a patient called me at home needing dermatological care at the office. Because Dr. Ulrich lived nearby, I asked my wife and daughter to accompany me so that we might visit Dr. and Mrs. Ulrich afterward. I wanted Marcy and our daughter, Emily, to hear Dr. Ulrich's life story, which he had shared with me during our lunch conversations. Dr. Ulrich had always said that I was part of his family and could visit him anytime. Although my wife was uncomfortable about dropping in unannounced, I had a feeling that it was important to see him. Dr. and Mrs. Ulrich's home was only a few blocks from my office.

As we walked toward his front door, twilight was approaching. We rang the doorbell and no one answered. After waiting several minutes, we started to leave, assuming that it was too late in the evening. When we got into the car, Dr. Ulrich appeared at his front door. He was a tall and distinguished-looking man. He smiled broadly and said, "I'm so happy to see you!" He ushered us into the living room with Mrs. Ulrich and I asked him to tell Emily and Marcy his life story. We sat for several hours and I could see that they were extremely interested in his life. Although I had heard these stories during our lunches together, I enjoyed hearing them again, as if for the first time. The following week, I spoke with Dr. Ulrich and told him how much we enjoyed spending time with him and Mrs. Ulrich. He remembered that I had always wanted Emily to hear his life story.

Several weeks after the visit, Mrs. Ulrich called me to relate that Dr. Ulrich had been admitted to Oakwood Hospital. Although he wasn't able to talk or see me in the hospital, I knew that he felt my presence and caring for him. I often think back to that phone call from my patient on Labor Day weekend, grateful that Emily and Marcy were with me on that Saturday so we could share an evening with the Ulriches. Dr. Ulrich passed away at Oakwood Hospital on November 11, 1997, at the age of 82.

For several months after his death, I felt a great loss. I thought of him each day, as I do now, for I missed my mentor and friend. I also missed his spiritual wisdom, caring and kindness. I remember getting up in the morning and going to work each day

Dr. and Mrs. Ulrich share special time with Emily Waldinger, May 1989

thinking that there was something unresolved. I didn't quite understand this feeling because I knew that Dr. Ulrich had lived a long and wonderful life and was at peace with himself and his God.

One morning I awoke and thought I had the answer. Although I possessed personal letters from Dr. Ulrich, I lacked a written description of his philosophy. I wished that I had asked Dr. Ulrich to write down his philosophy of life, along with his personal anecdotes that had contributed to or reflected his philosophical beliefs. As I entered my office, I wondered why it was so important to have had Dr. Ulrich write down his thoughts because he had shared these beliefs with me on numerous occasions.

Many months passed and I continued to struggle with this issue. Finally, I had the answer. I realized that some day I would no longer be practicing medicine in Dearborn, Michigan. Dr. Ulrich's death made me aware that my practice included many patients in their later years of life who had also shared the thoughts, joys and sorrows of their lives with me. I knew that I had limited time to learn their philosophies of life and the experiences that shaped each individual's perspective. These patients have also bestowed upon me tremendous kindness and warmth, which paralleled Dr. Ulrich's way of being. Moreover, I wanted to create a special tribute to Dr. Ulrich.

When Dr. Ulrich passed away, I struggled in my practice. I had lost my mentor and great friend. There were moments when I thought I should return to an academic department of dermatology to pursue research interests. I rediscovered the true meaning of medicine in the process of writing this book. I learned that one of the most important aspects of life is to seek wisdom from people in our lives. It has been particularly rewarding for me to seek the wisdom of older people. I have been able to do this with my patients and this forms the basis of this publication. The process of seeking wisdom from people creates a warmer, closer relationship and a connection that transcends the typical way that we interrelate. This search can lead to connecting with their spiritual essence.

In the process of seeking the wisdom of my patients, I learned more about Dr. Ulrich and about myself. I experienced significant positive changes as a person and noticed that issues that used to concern me are more easily faced. I realized that although the connection we have with our immediate family is of great importance, we can also have a significant connection with people we meet in the course of our lives. This type of connection can help us in a different way. It can be a source of new wisdom and support, thereby changing our view of ourselves and of life.

I will be forever grateful to my patients for their kindness and the time they have taken to share their philosophies of life with me. They have taught me that each person has a unique wisdom. If you are fortunate to learn that wisdom, it will enrich and change both of you. As a physician, you will have greater insight into your patient and a deeper understanding of him or her as a person. This creates a warmer, special relationship between the doctor and the patient. It also has the potential to be life-transforming.

The Wisdom of Life Through My Patients

The Spiritual Essence of a Person

At the conclusion of each day, I carefully review the charts of all patients and scheduled appointments. This includes charts from patients who were unable to come or who had to reschedule. My office staff writes a note on the chart if there is a known reason for the cancellation or no-show appointment so that I am aware of my patients' condition.

One evening as I was going through this daily ritual, I read that one of my patients had been seriously injured in a plane crash. I immediately called his home and spoke with a family member. She told me that he was critically injured and in a coma. During the next year, I called this gentleman several times to see how he was progressing. His recovery was protracted and difficult.

I saw this patient approximately one year after the accident. He was partially paralyzed, had a short-term memory loss and had difficulty communicating verbally. Nevertheless, he was extremely happy to see me. To my astonishment, he displayed the same robust smile and positive attitude that he possessed at each visit prior to the plane crash. I attributed his cheerfulness at this visit to being able to get out of his home, finally getting some fresh air, and coming to the office.

He returned periodically in the ensuing months for treatment of dermatological conditions. I again noticed that at each visit his cheerful spirit was no different than it was the first day I met him. I thought to myself that his significant medical problems had not changed his spiritual essence. This was certainly a most remarkable and courageous person. As we sat in the exam room, I wondered how he was able to maintain a courageous and positive attitude in the face of such adversity.

At first I hesitated to ask, but because he had always displayed such warmth, I felt comfortable asking him the following question: "It is amazing to me that after all that you have been through, you still have an optimistic attitude and warm smile. How are you able to do this?" He looked at me, smiled, and said, "Doc, I was a Marine. The difficult we do right away. The impossible takes a couple of minutes."

As we spoke for several minutes in the examination room that day, I told him how special he was and that he was an inspiration to me.

I continued to think about this individual throughout that day and into the evening. This was a person I had always enjoyed. But I had learned something unique about him, his philosophy of life, and had connected with his spiritual essence. This connection was important and held great meaning for me. I also knew that I had started that conversation with one question which I was initially hesitant to ask. Perhaps it was too personal. I was happy that I asked that question for it has enriched my life. At the end of our office visit, I knew that he was very comfortable sharing his thoughts with me. There had been many other times when I experienced special connections with patients. These incidents may not be as dramatic as this patient's story, but they are equally important.

I mentioned previously that when Dr. Ulrich passed away, I felt that there was something unresolved. I thought about this each day until I began this book. As I spoke with my patients about this book and requested their philosophy of life statements, something universal occurred. Each patient extended a special warmth and kindness to me. I thanked each one of them.

As I read their stories, I recalled the inspiring moment when my patient said, "The difficult we do right away. The impossible takes a couple of minutes." The process of seeking the wisdom of my patients often facilitated the ability to connect with their spiritual essence. The process of connecting with their essence opened the door to their wisdom. I began to realize that the spiritual essence and the wisdom of a person can be reflections of each other. When you seek one, you will find the other. The wisdom of a person can be life-transforming. Their spiritual essence can be life-comforting.

I discovered this observation when I was rereading my book. I noticed that when I was seeking their wisdom, I wanted to add that I was seeking their spiritual essence as well. I also observed that when I spoke of their spiritual essence, their wisdom came to mind. As you read, I think you will observe this connection as well.

As the book progressed, I noticed that many of my previous concerns and preoccupations vanished. Instead, I thought about the wisdom, kindness and optimism that my patients shared. I realized that making the effort to seek the wisdom of people one is close to can be life-transforming. Our lives become more meaningful. We become better fathers and mothers, husbands and wives, sons and daughters, friends and doctors.

As physicians, we become more aware of our patients. We are better able to communicate with them. Patients experience a greater comfort which forms a stronger doctor-patient relationship. In the process of using our medical knowledge to help our patients, we can be enriched by their wisdom. The changes that have occurred in modern medicine make it difficult to establish this kind of relationship. However, in my opinion, medicine can only be fulfilling when we take a personal interest in our patients, for only then will physicians have the opportunity to seek the wisdom of life through their patients.

There are certainly many wise and intelligent people who have great knowledge about philosophy and religion. I admire them and seek their wisdom. I believe that each of us in our own way can live a more satisfying and fulfilling life if we understand the value of seeking wisdom and connecting with the spiritual essence of people close to us. I have found that this is particularly rewarding if it is with people in the later years of their life. I hope that as you read these philosophies, you will appreciate the uniqueness and wisdom of my patients. Although they come from many different backgrounds and life experiences, their philosophies all have universal appeal.

I also hope that this book will create within you a lifelong interest to pursue wisdom from others in your daily lives. We all come from different parents, different places and different backgrounds. Each of us follows a unique path. Understanding the wisdom of a person can bridge our differences and help build a foundation for our lives. This can lead to a connection with his or her spiritual essence. It does not replace other important facets of your life; rather, it adds value, wisdom and comfort.

To my patients, thank you for contributing to this book. You have given me the gift of your wisdom.

*To My Children
Jason and Emily*

Every year as your birthdays approach, I sit down at my desk
and write you a special letter. This is and will continue to be
a very important tradition for me to follow. However, this year I
will write you a combined letter.

Part of my philosophy of life has been based on seeking wisdom from people who are older than me. I remember as a child
having long talks with my mother and father about the meaning
of life. In my teenage years, the use of public transportation
enabled me to have visits with my grandmothers. I recall sitting
with them, listening to stories about their lives and appreciating
their wisdom. Their kindness and love were always enjoyed as
well.

At the age of 17, I moved away from my family to begin my
studies at the University of Michigan. My decision to become a
physician was made at this time. I feel the same today at 44 as I
did at 17 about the choice of my life's work. It was through this
profession that I knew I would be able to dedicate my life to
helping others. I was also motivated because I was confident
that medicine would allow me to interact with many people in
their later years of life. This interaction has always been one of
my greatest joys.

This book reinforces the importance of gaining wisdom from older people and shows how we can benefit from it. This is more important to me now than ever before. Gathering and receiving information for this publication has had a greater impact on me than I had ever imagined. I am passing this on to you because I think it will help you in your lives.

Every time I received a philosophy of life statement from a patient, I would think about Dr. Ulrich and about both of you. I felt that it was extremely important for you to read these philosophies. I hoped you would learn a great deal from them. Both of you have taught me so much, and you are the joys of your mother's life and mine. Furthermore, I have tried to guide you and instill in you the best moral, ethical and religious beliefs that will protect you throughout your lives.

I would like to share with you something that I think will be very important in your lives. There will be moments when you will doubt yourself, make mistakes, or do something wrong. What you both must remember at this time is to seek the truth, seek wisdom from God, and seek wisdom from people you trust. Always be aware of yourself and the reasons for your actions.

The wisdom from my patients in this book will also help you. For example, the importance of perseverance is discussed by Miss Marjorie Cornell. The value of never giving up and accepting people and experiences is written about by Mr. John Griffin. Faith in God and love in your life are expressed in Mrs. Wanda Haywood's statement. Generosity and charity are stressed by Mrs. Marion Simmons. Strong family values and virtues, the need to trust, love, and show affection to your future wife or husband as well as faith in God were written about by Mr. and Mrs. Webber.

You have often heard me tell you that if you have nothing nice to say about someone, do not say anything at all. Mrs. Helen Lemke shares this belief with us. She also relates something that your elementary school principal said in her commencement speech in fifth grade. I am sure she gives this advice to each graduating class. If you remember, your elementary school principal told you how important it is to be positive toward other people, give of yourself, and maintain strong ethical values. She pointed out that going to middle school would be a challenge and a new experience. She stated that you would be successful and make many new friends if you followed her guidelines. She stressed that this would not only be important in middle school, but throughout your entire life. Mrs. Helen Lemke also writes, "If you give a little of yourself, you will get twice as much back." Always try to help someone and do your part. I promise that the rewards will be great. When there is too much pressure, just say a prayer. If that doesn't help, say another and then another. This is written differently than your elementary school principal's words, but the thought remains the same.

Mr. Lemuel Teague gives you excellent advice when he says, "My experience in life has taught me to trust my fellowman until he gives me reason not to." His grandfather once told him, "Wrong me once, shame on you—but wrong me twice, shame on me." This is how I have tried to live my life. There are many wonderful people in the world, but you also have to be aware that people can do you harm.

Dr. James Mendola writes that he attributes much of his success to his parents who never graduated from high school. "I am pleased to say that when I talk with my parents on the phone, we end each and every conversation with those three little words, 'I love you,'" states Dr. Mendola.

In the process of writing this book, I have discovered the importance of seeking wisdom and connecting with the spiritual essence of people in my life. I know that you both remember Dr. Ulrich well. I believe that this quality is one reason he was very special to his patients. There are so many patients who have shared with me the profound effect he had on their lives. Dr. Ulrich had this effect on me when we practiced medicine together and after he retired. My book shares this with you.

I could continue on to write about all the rest of my patients' philosophy of life statements, but I will let you read them for yourselves. I know that each one of them will enrich your life. I would recommend that you read them each year as your birthday approaches to set your course for the next year.

I want to end with the same words that Dr. Mendola always shares with his parents. . .

I love you both very much.

Dad

The Widsom of Life
Through My Patients

No one person has all the world's wisdom.
People everywhere share small pieces
whenever they share ideas.

– Ashanti Folk Tale

---❖---

Mr. John Griffin

*"As I grow older, I am trying to learn what really matters
in life. I fail most of the time, but at least I get up and try
again to really learn that love and acceptance of everyone
and every day and every experience are what really
count."*

I'm 73 years old, a widower, father of 10 children, and
grandfather of 17. I'm an adjunct professor of psychology
at the University of Detroit Mercy and, in addition, the execu-
tive secretary of a tool and die manufacturers association. I'm
in love with reading–more non-fiction now, and partially
addicted to that most frustrating of all activities golf–or, to be
more correct, my peculiar version of the game.

In my 73 years, my strongest memories are of the magnificent dignity which my wife, Ann, showed while suffering the
erosion of her body and mind to Alzheimer's disease. Second, I
also recall the courage displayed by my best friend and assistant squad leader, Carl Steinle, who was killed in action in
Germany in 1945. In seven months of combat, he was the only
man I ever saw who showed no fear in combat.

As I grow older, I have tried to learn what really matters in
life. I fail most of the time, but at least I get up and try again to
really learn that love and acceptance of everyone and every
day and every experience are what really count.

Tolstoy's *Where Love Is, There Is God* and *Death of Ivan
Ilyitch* teach me these truths each time I read these stories.
Now, two stories about Ann Griffin, my wife. She hadn't

spoken for two to three years—not a single word. Our son, Pat, who lived in San Francisco at the time, came to visit her. A few of us were in the room. The nurse said, "Look who has come to see you. Do you know him?" Ann said, "Yes. That's my son, Pat."

My second story about Ann was that four years later, four years of complete silence, four years of my visits three times a day, seven days a week, four years of talking and holding her and tending to her, four years of loving her even more than all of the years before, she looked at me as she often looked at me and, out of, or from deep spools of confusion, and a heaping-on of heavy layers of forgetfulness of a long-buried life of blankness, somehow these words fought through—the last words she ever spoke—only three words—"I love you." She was a magnificent woman.

Commentary:

When I began my practice with Dr. Ulrich in 1985, I noticed that he had a remarkable caring for each patient. In the five years that we practiced together, I appreciated his ability to understand and connect with patients of all ages. Many parents told me that their children would seek advice from Dr. Ulrich. He would take time to listen and help with any of their concerns. Many elderly patients shared with me that he was there for them in time of need. Dr. Ulrich was able to convey a fatherly love and acceptance to which each patient responded. This love and acceptance parallels Mr. Griffin's philosophy of life.

Mr. Griffin was the first person I spoke with about my interest in writing this book. He has been a patient of mine since 1989. Mr. Griffin is an avid reader like my father. He always tells me which book he is currently reading and recommends books for my father. This gentleman exudes a special warmth and kindness each time I see him. I am touched by his consistent interest in my father, a man he has never met.

After reading Mr. Griffin's eloquent words, I had a greater understanding and a better connection with him. I reflected on Dr. Ulrich's intuitive way of connecting with his patients.

Dr. Ulrich had a natural ability to make a connection with people. For those of us who may not be so innately gifted, there is another way to accomplish this. It simply involves taking time to ask a loved one, friend, or mentor what is important in life or what is his or her philosophy of life. It is more profound when you ask them to include personal experiences, people or events that helped form or reflect their philosophy of life. This process creates a greater understanding between two people and forever changes the relationship in a positive way.

Finally, to Mr. Griffin, I believe that the last three words spoken by your wife are a tribute to you and were heaven-sent.

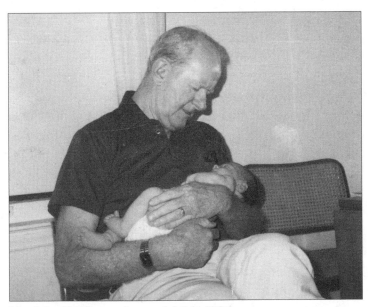

Mr. John Griffin and grandchild, 1994

Mrs. Wanda Haywood

"I pray that my grandchildren will always remember that the good will outweigh the bad and apply it to their lives. I pray that God will keep them in his protective care and when I have to leave here, they will know I am still here with them through my love for them."

I was born in a mining camp in a place called Green Castle in the rolling hills of West Virginia. Born Wanda Lee Jenkins, August 16, 1938, to a couple by the name of Gladys Faye Jenkins (Tincher) and Marion Sam Jenkins.

I was born in the mountains where you can stand and look over the valleys and see the rivers running for miles with streams of water flowing from the mountains. I remember snow-capped trees in winter and a picture postcard of colorful hues in the fall.

I sometimes go home on what is called Bridge Day on the New River Bridge at Fayetteville, West Virginia, where the bridge spans the river from one mountain to another. It is the longest single arch bridge in the world and people come from all over the world to parachute off the bridge that particular day.

My father, needless to say, was a coal miner. He started to work, crawling and digging his way through the mines, at the age of 9. My father was a hard-working man. He was a very good father. Every time we heard the whistle blow at the mines, we knew someone was in trouble. As a rule, that meant a cave-in or a fire. My dad was given up twice for dead from

Mrs. Wanda Haywood's parents, 1965

cave-ins, but God had other plans and spared his life for which we were very thankful. My mother was a wonderful mother. She took very good care of us. I have five sisters—Katherine Marie, Emmogene, Marleen, Drema Ruth, and Veronica Lynn. God called my dad home in 1980 and my mom in 1986.

I used to spend many hours in the company store where they eventually made the movie "Matewan." My dad worked for the coal company that owned this store. We would walk five miles to get scrip to buy food and goods from the store. Most of our food was homegrown or raised. My dad raised chickens and hogs and grew a garden. Our hams were hung to cure and we made our sausage and baked pork rinds. We also made our own lye soap.

I also remember when times were so bad that we would share a skillet of water gravy with the family from across the railroad tracks. Our Christmas tree was always cut and fresh, because they were always plentiful. We made what we could to decorate, but we never bought any decorations. Our stringing of popcorn was always fun. I walked miles to and from school in grades one through five. I shared with other students a one-room schoolhouse where our teacher would cook a pot of beans while she taught us and the potbelly stove warmed us. This same teacher taught our mother what education she had, which was not too many years, as she was married at the age of 14. My dad was a self-taught man who knew a little of every-thing.

Our life was a hard one, but a good one. I remember a very strict home that was always full of love and a lot of good times. We had an icebox and sometimes a truck would come by and we would buy a block of ice. That was a treat to have some-thing cold for a change. We also studied our homework by an old oil lamp. We had to carry our water from a spring or the pump we had to prime. We also caught rainwater to wash clothes and scrub the floors. We would use this same water to wash our hair to make it softer. We carried our coal and chopped our wood for our fireplace. There was no gas heat or electricity, at least not in our part of the country. We had an outhouse, as there was no indoor bathroom. We also had Saturday night baths in the big tub. We had a creek that ran behind our house, so we washed often.

Our dad would shovel a path from our house to the outhouse and the snow was so deep you would be afraid the snow would fall in and bury you alive. We had this footbridge which we called a swinging bridge. That was a good name for it because it really did swing. My mother washed clothes in a tub and on an old washboard. I saw her small hands bleed many a time as she did this and hung our clothes out to dry. She would stand and press them with an iron she had to heat on the old coal stove. And, I wonder now how she could have held so much love in her heart for all of us.

We used to string beans and hang them up to dry. They were called leather britches. We fixed these to be eaten in the wintertime. We picked blackberries and made cobblers, jams and jellies. I still do these every now and then, with the exception that I pay more attention to the snakes now than the berries.

On the Fourth of July, the company store would deliver a case of pop and two gallons of ice cream packed in dry ice. Our games were Marbles and Kick the Can. We also did this silly dance called the May Pole Dance.

I never knew either one of my grandfathers because they had passed on before I was born. I had two wonderful grandmothers. I still think of my mom's mother and how I used to go out in the yard and pick apples from the trees, sit under the Beechnut tree for hours, and run through the field of flowers. My mom would bake sweetbread that had an aroma that would make your mouth water. We would make snow ice cream, and listen to a radio that was powered by a car battery. I listened to "Boston Blackie," and "The Squeaking Door" and "The Grand Old Opry."

I often think of my mother, especially when I design a ballet costume for my granddaughters. I remember my mother's talents in the area of arts and crafts and how she encouraged me to follow in her footsteps. She used to make our clothes from the feedsacks she would save until she had enough of the same pattern. Or, we could order from the catalog, or buy from the old peddler who came by twice a year. I sure can relate to Loretta Lynn's song "The Coal Miner's Daughter" for I have been there. I sure had a lot of dreams when I was young, but a lot less money. Somehow the love replaced the money, and I have had a wonderful life.

At the age of 16, I met and married a wonderful man who was 19. He had gone into the Marines at the age of 16 and had just gotten out. His name is Frank Haywood. He has been a hard worker, a good provider, and loved me even when I couldn't love myself. Most of all he has always been my good friend. He was stricken with colon cancer in 1995, and hope was dim. By his faith and God's loving grace, he has extended our wonderful life to date.

We thank God daily for His many blessings. Frank and I thought—what is a missing colon and the rest that went with it. As long as we can have quality life and be together, we will take it and be forever grateful.

I love reading and teaching Sunday school to teenage girls. Frank and I also play a little music and sing. We have one child, a son Frank Haywood Jr. He designs houses and teaches college, works as an inspector, and is in construction development. But most of all he is a wonderful father to our precious granddaughters, Hillary Caitlin and Haley Lauren Haywood, and a good husband to our daughter-in-law, Julie. We thank God so much for them. Hillary and Haley have been the reasons for us to go on when we felt that we could not. We are very proud of our son and have an undying love for him, and thank him so much for our granddaughters.

I have enjoyed tracing our family roots. I searched for years and one day went to the Burton Historical Archive in Detroit and there found our family's book on a shelf. What a thrill when I saw my mom and dad's name there, and to know there were a lot of important people I was connected to. I pray that my grandchildren will always remember that the good will outweigh the bad and apply it to their lives. I pray that God will keep them in His protective care and when I have to leave

Bridge Day celebrated every year in Fayetteville, West Virginia

here, they will know I am still here with them through my love for them.

Soon I will celebrate my 60th birthday. My mind wanders back to a time in my life as a young girl when my five sisters and I endured a life of poverty as did many others. The only difference was the love we had to replace the poverty that made me a stronger person. Our mother was very strict, but always gave us the love we needed and her prayers have gone a long way. She always taught us to give love and kindness to our fellowman and it would always be returned to us.

This brings me to a very special man, Dr. Thomas Waldinger. I recall the first time I met him. I wondered if this doctor could be for real. I could feel a genuine concern and a love that had to be God-given. I remember when he told me that I had cancer on my nose. The earthly part of me was afraid for I had recently lost my father to cancer, but the spiritual part of me was at peace. Dr. Waldinger told me he could operate on me in the office or, if I wanted, he could send me to the hospital to have it done. I told him to operate on me in his

office, for I trusted and had faith in him and in God. I felt God
had everything in control. I felt at that time and still do to this
day that Dr. Waldinger is a precious soul that God leads daily.

Three years ago, my husband was stricken with severe colon
cancer which had spread and the prognosis was not good. But
thanks be to God, he is still here and enjoying our precious
granddaughters, Hillary and Haley. Also, we have four other
children whose lives God has allowed us to share—Jennifer,
Kassie, Andrew and Josh. We are not legally their grandparents,
but our hearts say they are ours.

Thank you, Dr. Waldinger, for all your warmth love and
understanding. I will always be grateful. May God bless you
and yours always. In God's love.

Commentary:

Wanda Haywood is a loving, special, sweet soul. I remember
so well the day that she came into the office and we discussed
the skin cancer on her mid-upper nose.

I reviewed with Wanda all of the therapeutic options. She
looked at me and said, "I have faith in God and faith in you
and only want you to perform the surgery." Her abiding faith
in me was inspiring.

Wanda had transformed me in a certain way. She affirmed
the importance of faith in God in our lives. As physicians, with
all our wisdom, skill and experience, we must remember the
influence of faith on our patients. We do not have to discuss
this, but it will be apparent to them.

When I asked Wanda to write her philosophy of life statement, I thought it was poetic and beautiful. I admired her even
more than that day many years ago in the office. Although a
genuine philosophical moment was shared with her then, I was
unaware of her background and philosophy. By reading
Wanda's story, I gained a much greater insight into her and
myself.

❖

Mrs. Marion Simmons

"I learned in childhood that everyone is respected, and we share what we have, however little it may be, with those who have less."

I lived and grew up in the 1930s in Philadelphia with my parents and sister. My parents had suffered losses in 1929 when the economy collapsed and many others did also.

In the early years of the 1930s, before I was in school, there were many peddlers coming to the house. They weren't beggars, as they had had homes and families and jobs, but were now homeless. They put together small sewing kits and kits of other small household items, so an exchange was made with a few pennies for a spool of thread or some pins. I remember the small pile of pennies that was kept on the table by the front door. No one was turned away empty-handed. Two or three pennies were given and a kind word. Sometimes on cold winter days, the peddler was invited in to get warm and have a small bowl of homemade soup. My mother listened well as they talked of their former lives.

When we were older and in school, our classmates were our friends and playmates. In winter, we went sledding, and when we were older we went ice skating on frozen ponds. In nice weather, we roller-skated—the skates were metal, clamped to one's shoes, and were tightened with a key. Double-Dutch jumping rope and an infinite variety of other activities that

Mrs. Simmons, 1988

children make up as they go along were enjoyed by us. The boys always seemed to play baseball. On rainy days, we played board games or cards in one or another's house. For us, growing up in the 1930s, it was the best of times. For adults, it was the Great Depression.

When we were older, we found that we could go anywhere in the city on our own and not be afraid. The city was very well kept and we liked it. It wasn't very crowded–traffic was slight, because everyone used the bus, trolley or elevated train/subway. As we expanded our horizons, we found that people were pleasant, considerate and polite. It was automatic to do "little acts of kindness." That was the way the country was.

The United States is very generous–whenever or wherever there's a need, there also is the country–with money, equipment and people to help. It takes care of its own and has social and welfare programs to aid those who need it. The country and the government are made up of people. So, they should act as we do.

I learned in childhood that everyone is respected, and we share what we have, however little it may be, with those who have less. We care about, and care for, our fellowman. It would seem then that living is generosity, and no one is left out or forgotten. There is no better way to live and not a better place in which to do it.

Commentary:

Mrs. Marion Simmons is a joy to see in the office because of her friendly and generous spirit. I am reminded of the kindness and generosity of Dr. Ulrich.

Approximately six years after Dr. Ulrich retired, I called him late one evening because there had been a tremendous downpour that night in Dearborn and water was leaking through the office windows. Dr. Ulrich volunteered to come over immediately with buckets and towels. He also told me that he would call Felix Pikulski, who has maintained our office for over 30 years.

Dr. Ulrich encouraged me to go home and rest because I faced a full schedule the next day and said he would "maintain the fort." I was extremely tired and very grateful for his help. I thought back to our first months together in practice when he refused to accept remuneration for his services. Although we had not practiced medicine together for six years, he continued to display the same generosity and kindness. I have tried to emulate these qualities in my life.

> "Humanitarianism is a link that binds together all Americans. . . .Whenever tragedy or disaster has struck in any corner of the world, the American people has promptly and generously extended its hand of mercy and help. Generosity has never impoverished the giver; it has enriched the lives of those who have practiced it. . . .And the bread we have cast upon the waters has been returned in blessings a hundredfold."
>
> – Dwight David Eisenhower

Mr. Joseph Koss

"We made paper footballs or taped up baseballs that were discarded by sandlot teams. These baseballs and footballs were used in 'real championship' games that far overshadowed today's World Series games or the Super Bowl."

It is difficult to place a value judgment on one's personal beliefs. The reason is that the influences of church, family and society combine to intermesh these values and blend them into a unique individual with unique personality characteristics. In fact, if I were to summarize these characteristics and draw from my lifetime experiences, I would have to say that a healthy individual would have to possess the virtues of good, prudential thinking that will discern right from wrong as well as love and compassion toward others.

In judgment of my life's work both as a supervisor at General Motors and later as an electrical instructor at Henry Ford Community College, I have found myself richly rewarded by working with people and helping them with some of their problems. In evaluating my personality and its development, I find that the love shown by my parents was a dominant factor. My parents immigrated to America in 1917 from the small state of Slovenia, Austria. Once settled in Detroit, they married and I am the youngest of their four sons.

I grew up during the Depression, which saw my father without work for seven years. Times were tough and survival seemed marginal at best. Fortunately, the combined unity and care-

Mr. Joseph Koss at daughter Diane's wedding reception, 1988

giving of families and neighbors made survival more of a certainty. The lack of monetary wealth seemed to manifest itself into family closeness and love. It created times of personal family humor as well as times of creative expression. I still recall having to make my own toys. An example of this was carving human shapes out of wood and making toy cars to park in cardboard boxes located beneath the furniture in the living room.

During the Depression, sports heroes were important to young minds. Trying to emulate these heroes led not only to creativity but also necessity. We made paper footballs or taped up baseballs that were discarded by sandlot teams. These baseballs and footballs were used in "real championship" games that far overshadowed today's World Series games or the Super Bowl.

Christmas was always a special time for us. The season started on December 6. That's when St. Nicholas would visit us and give a report to mom and dad on how good we had been during the year. If we were good, he would leave us a little gift—usually a bowl of fruit.

In later years, I would carry on this tradition with my own family by having them put their shoes outside their bedroom doors on December 6. This custom was used well into our children's teen years. In fact, I surprised my oldest daughter when she was a junior in college. On December 6, I located her car in the dorm parking lot and put a large boot filled with fruits and candy in it. The following morning, the response was immediate. My daughter called her mother asking where dad was last night. To this day, she relates to her friends the time when St. Nicholas visited her when she was in college and how significant it is to always put your shoes outside the bedroom door on December 6.

In the final analysis, I have lived a full life, a truly meaningful life in which I can credit the hard times for giving me a sense of humor and a respect for humanity.

Commentary:

Mr. Koss writes, "I can credit the hard times for giving me a sense of humor and a respect for humanity."

In his book *When Bad Things Happen to Good People*, Harold S. Kushner writes:

> "In the final analysis, the question of why bad things happen to good people translates itself into some very different questions, no longer asking why something happened, but asking how we will respond and what we intend to do now that it has happened. . . .the ability to forgive and the ability to love are the weapons God has given us to enable us to live fully, bravely and meaningfully in the less-than-perfect world. . ."

Mr. Koss' response to the hard times has allowed him to live a full and truly meaningful life.

Mr. Weslie Williams

"First child, bought first home and a car, and went to work for the first time in a factory."

As I look back on the decade of the '40s, more things happened then than any other decade I can remember. In 1940, my twin brother and I left Kentucky and headed for parts unknown in Detroit. It was there I got my first job. In 1941, when Japan attacked Pearl Harbor, war and the draft were utmost in my mind. Then, in 1942, I signed up for the draft and waited to be called. I got my call in 1943 and was sent to Fort Leonard Wood, Missouri.

Furthermore, in April 1944, I was married and, just two weeks later, was called to go to Camp Hampton Road in Virginia. There we were shipped to Oran, Africa. We stayed there until we shipped out to Italy. I traveled from the southern part of Italy to the north, before the war was over.

The year of 1945 brought the news that my daughter was born. It was good news because everything went well. Coming home, seeing my wife, my daughter and more of my family was really great later that same year. That year was a "first"–first child, bought first home and a car, and went to work for the first time in a factory. Nothing much happened until 1948 when we had another child, a boy. In 1949, I bought a brand new home and moved with the help of friends.

Mr. Weslie Williams, wartime photo, 1943

Sometime after I had been home for a while, my wife, Ora, showed me a letter she had received from the chaplain of our outfit. He wrote that I was OK. What he had written in that letter reminded me of the time my buddies stopped on a road in an old truck and a chaplain stopped to ask how we were. I thought it was unusual that an officer was seemingly searching us out. We talked a bit and then he was on his way. I never knew until I got home that he had received a letter from my wife and was looking for me. He had answered her letter.

Commentary:

At each office visit, Mr. Williams expresses great interest in me and my staff. His story reflects random acts of kindness that people do each day.

I have also been the recipient of these gracious gestures from my patients. My wife often says to our children, "Have you done any RAKs (random acts of kindness) today?" Wes, your wonderful story is at the heart of the goodness in people.

> ". . .The capacity to care is the thing that gives life its deepest significance."

> – Pablo Casals

Anonymous Patient

"High on the list of wonders is that of being able to associate with people of all sorts."

Your book about your patients' philosophies of life describes a project of enormous complexity! I imagine that you will receive a diverse collection of thoughts from your patients. It will be interesting to observe how you compile the many items into a coherent stream responsive to your proposed book title, *The Wisdom of Life Through My Patients*. I am sure that you can succeed. I wish you well.

You have asked me for a biographical note that might be supportive of my personal philosophy. Well . . . now . . . Thomas . . . my personal philosophy of life is still under construction and I am not sure that it is ready to be described in ink on paper. I can tell you a little about it but I am unable to state it in a simple few words. When it is ready to reveal, however, it will express my desire to help all with whom I have any association so that they will find only betterment of their lives from the association.

Just how this philosophical bent came to be mine I cannot say. Looking back I can recall some terrible moments that should have made me quite bitter in life. As a 5-year-old boy, I was abandoned by my mother. I can still remember the moment that she left our home. There was no one there except me at the time. It must have been as terrible a moment for her as it was for me. I remember that she promised to bring me an airplane when she returned.

My upbringing was left to my father and my grandmother. One winter and spring, the little country town of my school years fell victim to a siege of illness transmitted in the drinking water. Typhoid, diphtheria and scarlet fever killed one-third of the children in the town. I was afflicted with diphtheria and scarlet fever but I survived. I was left a not very well developed child who took a long time to recover. I became "bookish," according to my friends.

The Great Depression of the 1930s tested our little family. I didn't realize it at the time, but it was teaching me how to survive in a very low economic scale. High school was an awakening for me and I enjoyed every one of its facets. One of the teachers took a special interest in my case and to my delight was instrumental in my obtaining a four-year scholarship at a prestigious university. It was a tough struggle but four years later I graduated with honors. I found a wonderful girl as a loving wife and we started a family. A career in Electrical Engineering and Applied Physics was well under way when World War II took over. My time in service was short but it had been a soul-searing event. My wife had preserved the family while I had been away. I came home and wrapped myself up in their love. She was a lifesaver.

Now, what can be said about my philosophy? Thomas, I have every reason to be less than generous in my attitude toward life. But strangely, it is just the opposite. My Creator has, I believe, tested me more than once. But, He gave me recuperative powers that have carried me through some rough times. In addition, He gave me a wonderful and loving wife who has tolerated my lifestyle with grace.

My philosophy? Frankly, Thomas, it is very simple. To be alive and able to appreciate the wonders of Creation is a pleasure for me. High on the list of wonders is that of being able to associate with people of all sorts. I receive much personal pleasure in communicating with people. When first I meet someone, I enjoy evaluating the nature of the contact. At first the contact is a guarded one. It is as though one is viewing the new contact while being shielded behind a protective screen. Then as the nature and intent of the contact are made clear, the screen becomes less and less restrictive (or more so) as one's judgment commands. It is a kind of game. As the screen becomes less restrictive, the association becomes more productive. One must remember that each individual is a very complex product of our Creator's genius and it is a real privilege to have an unguarded exchange with each of them. There is something to be learned from every one of His Creations.

Your project is worth the effort, Thomas, and I wish you success with it. I know that its successful completion will give you much satisfaction. A greater reward will come, however, if it gives some reader a better understanding of the path of life designed for us by our Creator.

Commentary:

The wisdom in this patient's philosophy of life gives keen understanding of the path designed by our Creator and will help many others. His sentiments are most touching.

> "Life's greatest achievement is the continued remaking of yourself so that at last you know how to live."

> – Winfred Rhodes

❖

Mrs. Pat Barnes

"I figure that life has three very important elements: time, energy and memory."

It ain't the life, it's the liver," said Mother Alphonsine, the Mistress of Novices. I was 19 years old and had been in the convent for one year. After nine months as a postulant I had received the beautiful blue habit of the Sisters, Servants of the Immaculate Heart of Mary–a blue habit and a white veil. In two years I would take the vows of poverty, chastity and obedience and be allowed to wear the black veil of a professed sister.

The convent gets a lot of bad press. When I hear people talk about dried-up old nuns with a mean streak and a semi-automatic wooden ruler, I wish they could have had a peek inside Mother Alphonsine's novitiate.

She was a tall, big-boned woman in her 50s. Her posture was impeccable and her glasses as thick as coke bottles, but she had a smile that lit up a room and warmth that put even the most nervous novice at ease.

During recreation hour she could be talked into a demonstration of Irish step dancing or, and this was our favorite, she would read to us. There was one particular story, I think it was called *Mosquito Ranch*, that got her laughing so hard tears ran down her cheeks. She'd have to stop reading, pull off those thick glasses and wipe her eyes. Sometimes we were all laughing so hard at her and at the story that she just plain couldn't continue.

Mother Alphonsine had a motto for every occasion. When I bumped into the Christmas tree and a lovely glass ornament crashed on the highly polished tiles, her immediate response was, "Sic transit gloria mundi." (Thus passes the glory of the world.) If a novice seemed lonesome or down in the dumps, you could count on Mother Alphonsine to say, "A smile is cheaper than electricity, and it makes the home much brighter." She had volumes of these little snippets of wisdom on the tip of her tongue, but my very favorite was, "It ain't the life, it's the liver."

At first it stuck in my mind because the flawless grammar of our novice mistress had been invaded by the unspeakable "ain't." It was a good attention getter. As I pondered the meaning of the saying, I came to understand some of what she was teaching. Every person's life is packed with choices and challenges. You make your life what it is by what you choose to focus on. Like editors, we build up the scenes we select as important and minimize or forget what we don't want to be part of our life, our masterpiece.

I figure that life has three very important elements: time, energy and memory. It's up to us to decide how we will spend our precious time and energy and what memories we will either dwell on or downplay. I think this is how we build our lives, and I am so grateful to Mother Alphonsine for the funny little saying that started me thinking in this direction.

I left the convent after 10 years. It was a peaceful parting, no bitterness, and no rancor. On the contrary, I am grateful for the excellent education I received, for the wonderful women I met, and especially for the time I was given to think.

Mother Alphonsine died about five years ago. I think she must have been well into her 80s. She had been responsible for the formation of hundreds of young novices, all of whom are now eligible for AARP. I wonder how many of them remember, "It ain't the life. . . ."

Commentary:

When I talked with Mrs. Barnes about my book, she exhibited the happiest smile and expression. She then shared with me that she is a writer of children's books and hopes someday to publish one of her own. Mrs. Barnes writes in the early morning before work, as I do. There have been so many coincidences since I started this book that almost every day something special occurs in this vein.

In the preface of the book *Small Miracles*, Dr. Bernie Siegel writes: "I believe that *nothing* is a 'coincidence.' It's all part of creation and God's plan and our response. We just have to be open to seeing it. We have to want to see it and participate in creation. . . .

"A common coincidence that I experience all the time is that I find pennies wherever I go. When I enter a hotel room for the first time and it's been freshly cleaned, vacuumed, spotless, I can often count on finding a penny on the threshold. In the airport, in a restaurant, even sitting atop my luggage, I'll suddenly spy one solitary penny. Now, what does that mean? What does it say on a penny? 'In God We Trust.'. . .

"Here's another example: My wife and I own a cat named Miracle, and we decided to get her some company. A neighbor's cat had a litter of kittens and we were invited to choose one of our liking. I brought an adorable-looking kitten back home, but he and my wife didn't hit it off. The match didn't work out, and I had to bring him back to the original owner. My wife was sorry but the owner assured us there was no problem, all the other kittens had already been adopted—all, that is, except one. Somehow, no one seemed to like this last one, because she had grown up in a barn, was dark-brown, and very fearful of people.

"'Oh, what's her name?' I asked and the owner answered casually, 'Penny.' I hadn't been planning to try the experiment a second time, but the minute I heard the name, I knew it was right. So we adopted Penny. . ."

I am sure that Mrs. Barnes believes that Mother Alphonsine was not a coincidence in her life.

❖

Miss Marjorie Cornell

"My parents shared with others in need and this was 'passed on' to me."

My philosophy to persevere started as a child in a 20 by 20 foot home that my father built during the Depression. It was located in the country three miles west of Ann Arbor. The fabric of my life was formed by:

- Being responsible for chores and working in the yard, garden and fields;
- Walking one mile to a one-room school through grade eight;
- Caring for my grandfather nights, arising at 5 a.m., walking 1/2 mile to get a ride into Ann Arbor, walking another mile to high school and reversing the process after school;
- Working six nights at St. Joseph's Mercy Hospital while carrying a full load of classes at the university;
- Teaching and graduating from the University of Michigan with a master's degree were the result of persevering and reaching goals.

My parents shared with others in need and this was "passed on" to me. Besides teaching for 36 years, many vacations were spent sharing in Appalachia, on Indian reservations, 11 times in Haiti and culminating with a summer of participating in youth camps around the world. Now in retirement, I find it is still a pleasure to share with others in various ways.

As other challenges have come by way of surgeries and cancer, I have sought the help of the Lord and persevered as in previous years. Each day it seems good to keep the yard beautiful, work with wood projects or travel.

Friends during the different periods of my life have been a blessing by encouraging, going along to share in various projects, being available in times of illness and sharing the joys of life.

The Lord is my source of life and my source for living a fulfilling and joy-filled life.

Miss Marjorie Cornell, elementary school teacher, 1990

Commentary:

One of my elderly patients shared with me that Miss Marjorie Cornell is "the best friend a person could have in the world." She is unable to drive and Miss Cornell always brings this patient to my office for medical care.

I am so impressed with Miss Cornell's philosophy of perseverance, friendship and faith. She continues to follow these principles in every stage of her life. She will always be a source of perseverance and faith for me.

"Perseverance opens up treasures which bring perennial joy."

– Mohandas Karamchand (Mahatma) Gandhi

Mrs. Florence Loriaux

"We are always together no matter what."

I was born in Detroit, Michigan, and have one brother and two sisters. I attended three Catholic schools and met my husband some years later. Albert was born in Bricknell, Indiana, and came to Michigan with his parents when he was 6 years old. He went to school and worked to help his mother and father. Then he went into the Navy for about three years.

Yes, I knew Albert before he went in after World War II was over. In 1946, three months after he came home, we got married. We had five beautiful children—three boys and two girls. Three of my children live just a few miles from us. My youngest son lives just a block away. When my children were small, we often went on picnics with my husband's family and sometimes with mine. When they got older, we joined a bowling league for a few years. Then we all went camping. Our children do not bowl too much any more, except for one of my grandsons. He is really into it and would like to be a pro bowler.

We have 11 grandchildren and six great-grandchildren. We sure do have a good family. Albert had worked for one of the Big Three automakers. In 1986 or 1987 he had a new hip put in on the right side and had to retire from work. In the meantime, he got skin cancer from being in the sun too much. His skin is

Florence and Albert Loriaux, 50th wedding anniversary celebration, September 1996

very light. In 1992, he went into the hospital. We thought it was his heart. Well, we were told he had chronic leukemia of the blood. In 1998, he had a new knee replacement on the left leg.

Yes, my husband has been in and out of hospitals for one thing or another from skin cancer to having new parts put into him. Now, he has to have his eyes taken care of sometime in September 1998. We are always together no matter what. He is always with me and I'm always by his side when he needs me. When he is sick, I'm there. If he needs me with his woodcraft, I'm there to help. If he needs nursing, I'm there to nurse him back to health. He also does the same if I need his help. We are always together. Never alone. This year, 1998, we will be married 52 years, and still happy.

Commentary:

To new members of my staff, I have introduced both of you, Albert and Florence, as good friends. You respond that I am family to you. Over the years, you have made me feel that I am part of your family. You have shared family portraits, home-baked goodies, and your handmade artwork with me. It is wonderful to see you always come together to the office.

Your personal philosophy, always helping each other in life, sets a great example for all of us. You not only take care of each other, but you extend yourselves to people you meet.

There is no greater mission than someone reaching out to another.

> "He who wishes to secure the good of others, has already secured his own."

> – Confucius

Mrs. Dorothy McInerney

"The one thought that continually remains with me is that you should always have faith in God and believe in the power of prayer."

I am 81 years old, have five children and six grandchildren. I met my husband-to-be in the spring of 1941. Bernard was in the Army at that time, so we didn't date too often. In October of 1941, he was released from the Army because he was over the age of 28. However, he was ordered back into the service on February 7, 1942. Two months later, he was on a troop ship to Iceland for training. For 39 months, our only means of communication was via the mail. This is when he was in the European Theatre. Most of our letters, I believe, got through the German blockage because the ships sailed in convoys. When the war in Europe ended, he returned quickly because he had so many "points" to his credit. We were married for over 50 years.

In my lifetime, I have been privileged to know two people whose lives were personally affected by World War II and who have had an impact on my life. One was a French woman. This woman was imprisoned because her husband was very active in the French resistance. Her eldest son, Jean, who was about 18 at the time, also left home and joined a group of underground resistance. He killed a German officer and escaped, but the Germans found out. This boy eventually linked up with the U.S. Army and was attached to my fiancé's unit. He was killed at

Dornot (outside Metz). My fiancé wrote to the family and told them all the facts he could regarding Jean's death. That is how we eventually became acquainted with his mother. The SS troops of the German Army came to her summer home outside of Paris and arrested her. She was taken away and sent to a work camp. In the meantime, her husband was also arrested and died of hunger in Buchenwald. She learned about her husband's and her son's deaths when she returned to Paris at the end of the war.

Bernard and Dorothy McInerney with first child,
1946

The other person was a Roman Catholic priest of the Byzantine Rite. He was Romanian, married, with two daughters. He was forced to leave his country alone. He and his wife were separated for 17 years. She eventually was allowed to join him in the United States. He hadn't seen his daughters for many years. They both had married, and he had two grandchildren he had never seen. These people never lost faith and managed to survive and live useful lives.

The two families I mentioned, and their experiences during the war and after, enabled me to have a personal relationship with people who had actually suffered both physically and emotionally because of the war. Every morning I would read the paper and learn the latest news regarding the progress of the war, but it was impersonal. Knowing these two families brought me closer to the realities. Instead of reading about them, I actually could talk to them and learn about their experiences firsthand. It also made me realize how fortunate I was. Although this was a terrible experience for all of us who had loved ones in action, it seemed to me that it was not a time for self-pity because there were 10 million men and women from the U.S. who were in the service, so no one was unique.

The one thought that continually remains with me is that you should always have faith in God and believe in the power of prayer. I try to do this and many good things have happened in my life. I have survived cancer for almost 12 years. My family is very close and we keep in touch constantly. We enjoy one another!

As for my grandchildren, the only advice I would give them would be to stand up for the principles they have been taught—and to *keep a sense of humor*!!

Commentary:

Mrs. Dorothy McInerney is a graceful and elegant woman. She writes, "The one thought that continually remains with me is that you should always have faith in God and believe in the power of prayer."

In my ninth year of practice, my daughter developed juvenile rheumatoid arthritis. I remember praying to God each morning and evening for her recovery. Many of my patients intuitively knew that I was enduring a personal hardship and inquired about my well being. Each one of them was genuinely concerned and offered that Emily would be in their prayers.

These prayers of my patients during my daughter's illness were of immeasurable comfort. Emily completely recovered from her illness. Almost six years have elapsed, yet almost every month at least one patient will inquire about Emily's health. I always look into the patient's eyes and smile and, for a special moment, I remember the prayers and faith in God that my patients shared with me.

Mrs. McInerney also talks about something so essential to life, having a sense of humor. During my 40-minute commute to and from work, I listen to the radio. One morning there was an hour-long debate between the host and callers about whether golf was a sport. I laughed when one of the callers exclaimed that golf was clearly a sport because you could get injured.

In the middle of my morning that same day, I saw Mr. Lou Baker, an avid golfer, who had a cast on his arm. We always discuss golf during his visits. Mr. Baker has even shown me the proper grip, swing and stance. This is quite a feat in my small examination room because Mr. Baker is approximately 6 feet 2 inches tall, and there is not much room for him to demonstrate his technique. Seeing Mr. Baker's cast and thinking about the morning radio show, I asked if he had injured his arm playing golf. He looked at me and said, "Doc, I fell on a hickory nut at the golf course and fractured my arm." I then told Mr. Baker about the golf debate on the radio, and we shared a good laugh. Humor is such an important part of our lives. Each time I see Mr. Baker I remember this event and smile.

Mr. & Mrs. Cy Webber

"My parents set the example of love and consideration for each other that I have been able to use as a pattern to follow in my own life and marriage."

From the advantage of 73 years on this old earth, I have many rich memories that have brought beauty into my life. I was born in a very small town. At least it was a small town when I entered it–Preston, Idaho. Because of the Depression, we moved from Idaho to Kentucky. My youth was spent in those years called the Great Depression. Even though those years were hard ones, they were happy ones for me. While my dad never made a lot of money, he loved his family and we did a lot together. Family walks were one of our adventures. On other occasions, my mother would make a picnic and we would go to the park for an afternoon of fun and food. Once a month, if we could afford it, dad would take the whole family to Moka's Restaurant. The owner, Harry, was a good friend of dad's, and would always give us little goodies along with our meal.

My parents set the example of love and consideration for each other that I have been able to use as a pattern to follow in my own life and marriage. I was taught very early in life about the importance of God as a partner in life and of the many blessings we could receive if we followed His teachings. The teachings of Isaiah and of the Psalms became important to me. I remember that when I was in junior high school, a man used to come to the school once a month to our class and challenge us to memorize passages of scripture. We would get a dime for every verse we memorized. The first scripture I memorized was the 23rd Psalm because of its many verses (many to me as a youth). Therein began my love for the scriptures and the book of Psalms.

I met Glenna at Eastern Michigan University. We were married in our junior year and completed college together. We both entered the teaching profession and are now retired, having spent 30 years in a profession that has kept us young. We both taught at the high school level, dealing for the most part with wonderful teenagers. We have two sons and seven grandchildren and all live close to us and we see them often. Both sons are successful in their employment and are a joy to have near us. On April 15, 1998, we celebrated our 46th wedding anniversary.

Now, after 46 years of marriage, I look back at the events in my life and realize the opportunities that have come to me have come because of the values and virtues I was taught and was willing to follow. We have learned the need to completely trust each other, to show love and affection for each other–even in front of our children so they can see we are not ashamed of the love we share. We plan and do many things together. Though we have had many challenges in our married life, our trust in God and our ability to "roll with the punches" have given us the resilience to enjoy this beautiful world, even in adversity.

Commentary:

One Friday at the end of the day, I talked with Mr. and Mrs. Webber. They were so gentle, respectful and sincere with each other, a living example of what marriage should be. I was impressed that they were at peace with their lives and with each other. I am sure this is based on their values and virtues.

Mr. and Mrs. Webber shared another family event during this conversation. They were teachers and always made time to be in attendance at their children's sporting events. One day Mr. Webber was late to a swimming meet and when he arrived, his son was in last place. He was able to make eye contact with his son and give him a "thumbs-up" signal. Mr. Webber's son then proceeded to go from last place to first place in his remaining dives. What a profound effect a father's love and attention can have on his children.

At the end of our talk that afternoon, Mr. and Mrs. Webber were on their way to a grandchild's football game. The tradition continues.

Glenna and Cy Webber, newly engaged, August 1952

Mrs. Mary Lou Gorham

*"The time spent thinking and sorting out things at this time
in my life has helped me beyond words of expression."*

Outside, it's a beautiful Michigan summer day. Inside me, it is stormy and mixed with so many different emotions and feelings. When I was asked to put a few thoughts down to share with others, I chuckled and said, "Why me—especially at this time of turmoil?"

Our older brother lost his wife to pancreatic cancer four weeks ago. This week news came that our other brother has colon cancer. We are on our way now to Missouri as a family, to be with him and his wife for his surgery. Mom is scheduled for a repeat of surgery she had last summer. Instead of being another job I wasn't sure I had the time or energy for, writing this gave me the opportunity to put things back in place, restore my faith, and continue on. I thank you, Dr. Waldinger, for this. A calming has returned within me.

I have a loving, understanding husband and friend of 45 years. Daily, Robert goes beyond the call of duty for his family and friends. We have two outstanding daughters and one son. Also, we have three lovely grandchildren, young in years and trying to find their way in life. So many wonderful blessings to be thankful for.

Our mother is known as the "Angel Lady" at the senior apartment building where she lives. She makes and gives away angels by the hundreds. These are made and given with love to those she knows or just meets at a particular time or place in a person's life. Everyone who has met her, or has had the opportunity to know her, even briefly, will never forget her. She will be in their hearts forever.

By the way, her name is Okla Wales. Perhaps you have been blessed to have known her. In her quiet way, she truly is an angel walking here on earth amongst us. We love her.

The time spent thinking and sorting out things at this time in my life has helped me beyond words of expression. Thank you, Dr. Waldinger, for this opportunity to write about my thoughts.

Commentary:

I agree with Mrs. Gorham that her mother, Okla Wales, who is also a patient of mine, is an angel on earth. She is a sweet, kind and loving person. All of us are blessed and uplifted when we encounter people who display heartfelt kindness for the sole purpose of doing good.

When I read Mrs. Gorham's letter, I was delighted to learn that an effort devoted to honor my mentor had provided an opportunity to calm another person. Who knows how many times each of us in the process of doing good deeds may help others in unanticipated ways?

Since this writing, Mrs. Okla Wales passed away.

IN MEMORIAM

Mrs. Okla Wales
March 6, 1911–November 22, 1998

Mrs. Helen Lemke

*"When there is too much pressure—I just say a prayer.
If that doesn't help, I just say another, and another."*

I was born in 1915. The place was Yukon, Pennsylvania. It was a coal-mining town. My parents came from Poland. My father came first in 1900, and my mother, brother and two sisters came six months later. None of them could speak English. My mother couldn't read or write. She never went to school. She had four daughters and seven sons. My parents gave us a lot of love. I don't ever remember being hungry. We were a happy family.

I didn't get much schooling. I wanted to be a schoolteacher so much. Fifth grade was all I got. I started to work at the age of 9-1/2. I worked in a butcher shop and I didn't work full time. I got my working papers at the age of 12. My mother didn't want her boys to work in the mines, so we all moved to Hamtramck, Michigan, the year of 1928. I got a job three days after we got there working as a dishwasher in a restaurant. I got $1 per day, 12 hours of work a day, and no days off. I had to work—the Depression hit. It was hard and I gave up school to help. My dad wouldn't take welfare. He was in his 70s and got a job as a nightguard. When the school census came to check the students, my mother felt bad. She told them I was a niece who was just visiting.

In 1933, I met my husband, a Detroit police officer. I was 18, and he was 28. We were married for 58 years when he died. Clyde retired as a police lieutenant. We had three sons and one daughter. The three boys went to the Vietnam War. I'm so grateful because they all came back home. My oldest was a lieutenant colonel in the Air Force.

Sometimes people ask me about my way of thinking. I feel like I'm the luckiest person in the world. My parents were very loving. My three sons came home from the war. I have a wonderful daughter. They married wonderful people, and I treat them like my own kids. They make my sons and daughter happy. There's nothing I wouldn't do for them. I'm very open. "If I can't say something nice. . ." I like to see people happy.

I had a wonderful husband whom I loved very much to the end. I know he felt the same way about me. I love people. I don't care if they are black or white. I just look at life differently. We all were blessed and put here on this earth. It is up to us to be good or bad. All the good Lord does is give us strength and courage whenever we need it. No matter how bad we think we feel—it could be worse.

When I meet another senior citizen, it seems like we say, "The Golden Years—where are they?" They're here! Just open your eyes and look around. If you give a little of yourself, you will get twice as much back. Try to help someone. Do your part. I promise it will come out twice as good. When there is too much pressure—I just say a prayer. If that doesn't help, I just say another, and another. You'd be surprised how much it helps. It takes the pressure off.

P.S. I have 11 grandchildren and seven great-grandchildren.

Commentary:

"If you give a little of yourself,
you will get twice as much back.
Try to help someone. Do your part.
I promise it will come out twice as good."

— Mrs. Helen Lemke

"If I can stop one Heart from breaking,
I shall not live in vain
If I can ease one Life the Aching
or cool one Pain

Or help one fainting Robin
Unto his Nest again
I shall not live in Vain."

— Emily Dickinson

Mr. Carley Tolliver

"I believe our lives should be lives of service–that we owe to our Creator a responsibility to all mankind as well as to the earth upon which we live."

I was born December 11, 1931, in Whitaker, Kentucky. It is a small town between Hazard and Pikeville. The post office was South East Coal Company. I was the second of nine children. I grew up in a rural farming area raising hogs, chickens and growing most of our own food. I learned how to raise and care for animals and to grow a variety of crops.

My father had an ice business, and part of my responsibilities was helping him with ice delivery to both homes and businesses. I had all the childhood diseases in early school years and missed a lot of school due to sickness. I was always the smallest and skinniest kid in my school class. I weighed only 98 pounds in high school.

I believe our lives should be lives of service–that we owe to our Creator a responsibility to all mankind as well as to the earth upon which we live. Each person should leave this earth a better place than he or she found it. A life should have a positive rather than a negative factor. If the peoples of this world were true brothers and sisters as God intended, we could eliminate many of the problems in the world today. This type of interaction would benefit not only people, but plants and animals as well. Very few of us see all the beauty in God's creation.

Mr. Carley Tolliver, avid photographer, surveys father-in-law's peach trees, 1983

I remember when I was very young (during the ending of the Great Depression), I became aware of my responsibility to others. My father brought a young man home for dinner. This man had left his home looking for work because his parents and his family were desperately in need. My mother cooked an excellent dinner and, as we ate, with tears he told his story and expressed how wonderful it was to find people as kind as my parents. She always had a gift of listening and being able to cheer the hearts of those in need. As I listened, I became more and more conscious of the needs of others and developed great pride in my parents. I realize that I have patterned my life to always be aware of the needs of others. My parents (mostly my father) helped the young man find a job.

Our family was very religious, and I followed their example. Sunday morning at our house, as with many rural-mountain people of eastern Kentucky, found us preparing for a day of church-going and religious devotion. We always had guests for Sunday dinner, and I enjoyed listening to their conversations and learned more about people.

Moreover, my mother possessed a sense of cheerfulness and humor, which I also developed as I matured. She was always helping in the community to get help for the needy. Also, there was always company at our house and my mother listened and helped by collecting clothing for the needy, caring for the ill and preparing and taking food to neighbors who were unable to prepare their own food. Many people called on my mother to pray for them and to sit with the bedridden, etc. She could get more done in the community than anyone I ever knew.

In my junior high school years I attended Hindman Settlement School in Knott County, Kentucky. This school was famous for what I already believed–a life of service. Several nights during the week, great speakers would come to the Great Dining Hall, and after the evening meal, would give a short talk, and sometimes a long speech. We had good speakers who helped to mold my life and made my beliefs more steadfast.

During this time I became acquainted with a great man in my estimation–the Reverend J. S. Bell. I considered him to be totally dedicated to his work. He never retired, but continued his ministry until his death a few years ago. His taped messages are still played on radio stations in that area. Also, the founder of the Settlement School, Elizabeth Watts, further influenced my life. She always let me know that I was on the right track, so to speak.

I attended Caney Junior College at Pappa Passes, Kentucky. This was a small, nondenominational college in Knott County. Its founder, Alice Lloyd, was another great influence on my life. She was, furthermore, totally dedicated to the service of others. The college stressed what they called "The Purpose Road"–a life of service. Mrs. Lloyd sponsored many students who went on to the University of Kentucky at Lexington. She is responsible for many doctors, lawyers, teachers, ministers, etc. She never retired, but worked all these years as an invalid until her death. Mrs. Lloyd is listed in the "Who's Who" of dedicated women. She was on the Ralph Edwards television show "This is Your Life." Even today, Dr. Ralph Edwards serves as Trustee Emeritus on the Board of Trustees of the college.

With all these influences in my life, how could I believe or develop any differently than I have? All in all, it's the daily little things one does that really count. I met my wife, Josephine, at Caney College and she has a similar philosophy in life, so we have a lot in common. Our life together has been wonderful. We both feel that we have been positive factors in the world.

Commentary:

There is nothing nobler than Mr. Tolliver's mission: a life of service. At each office visit, Mr. Tolliver brings me an envelope. Inside this envelope are handwritten stories to share with my family. These stories are always humorous and enjoyed by all. It is very meaningful to me that he takes the time to do this.

The wisdom that he writes is practiced every moment of each day. Mr. Tolliver says, "It's the daily little things that really count." The world is a better place with Mr. Carley Tolliver in it.

"The sole meaning of life is to serve humanity."

– Leo Tolstoy

Mr. Lemuel Teague

"My experiences in life have taught me to trust my fellow-man until he gives me reason not to."

I was born 73 years ago in north central Texas. My father was a farmer, who took sick in December 1924. We moved to west Texas in 1927 where my father ran a small country store and gas station. We moved back to north central Texas in 1929 where we lived in a small house on my grandparents' farm. I had two older brothers and a younger sister. In 1933, we moved to a small valley just opening up in the upper Rio Grande region where my father received five acres of land for helping build an irrigation canal. My father died in 1934 in the middle of the Depression.

My mother was a seamstress. When I was nine, my sister and I had to go to work. My older brothers went out on their own. I worked for a truck farmer who raised strawberries and cantaloupes and then sold the Grit newspaper on weekends. I rode my bike about 40 miles each Saturday, delivering the paper. I learned to cook and prepare breakfast almost every day. We were living in town at this time. After my father died, we lost our house to a tornado, and my mother traded the five acres for two lots in town. We moved back to west Texas in 1939 where I worked for a grocery store every day before and after school and on Saturdays. In the summer, I worked for an electrician during the time I would normally be in school.

Mr. Lemuel Teague, his wedding day, 1954

In 1942, I turned 17 in May and enlisted in the Navy in July. During WWII, I served 26 months in the Pacific, flying in every kind of plane the Navy had. I was discharged in November 1945. I worked as an electrician from the time I was discharged until April 1950, when the Navy recalled me for the Korean War. For three years I taught classes in Equipment and Navigational Radar. I then foolishly re-enlisted and was assigned to a patrol squadron in anti-submarine warfare work. I have a total of 13 years in the Navy, on active duty flying for most of the time.

After Navy duty, I went to work for the FAA where I worked on navigational equipment and then on radar for tracking planes. So, you see, I was brought up by the school of hard knocks. However, I did manage to get three years of college, earning an Associate Degree in Electronics.

My experiences in life have taught me to trust my fellowman until he gives me reason not to. My grandfather once told me, "Wrong me once, shame on you–but wrong me twice, shame on me." So, that is how I have tried to live my life. I find there is some good in most people and they will treat you as you treat them. So, if you present your pleasant side to them, it will bring out the good side of them. I have lived in Texas, Virginia, California, Maine, Ohio and Michigan. I have found most people every place are the same–maybe a little more reserved in the cities. I now live in the country. Since I lost my wife, I spend my days golfing and fishing.

Commentary:

When Mr. Lemuel Teague first came to the office, I felt a warmth from him instantly. I sensed he was interested in other people and would always do his best to help anyone. He always exudes a grandfatherly kindness to me. I have often noticed in my practice that the similarities between people are much greater than the differences. I echo Lemuel's sentiment that people are the same all over the world. His philosophy is a key to greater understanding and world peace. If we attempt to locate common ground among us, we can form a bridge.

Mr. Teague offers great advice for children and young adults when he says, "Wrong me once, shame on you–but wrong me twice, shame on me." This provides one element for forming friendships and coping with peer pressure.

❖

Mrs. Sophie Kalmar

"Have a good day, and let every day be a good day for you and yours."

Love is a many splendored thing.

Love is one of the facts of life.

Love has a special meaning when you have someone with whom to share tears as well as laughter, tears as well as dreams, and silence when the time for words is past.

Love is having trust in others, and they having trust in you.

Love is having forgiveness for one another.

Love thy neighbors and your neighbors will share their love with you.

Love will bring happiness for family and many friends.

Family and friends will share their love and happiness with you.

Love does not always mean passion.

Commentary:

When I spoke to Mrs. Kalmar about my book, she said she was not sure what to write. I told her that she should write from her heart and that she is special to me. At the end of each visit Mrs. Kalmar always says to me, "Have a good day, and let every day be a good day for you and yours."

Sophie, you should know that although every day is a good day, it is a little more special when you are in it! Your poem is wonderful and so are you.

I would like to share with Sophie and all of you a story that Pema Chödrön writes in *The Wisdom of No Escape and The Path of Loving-Kindness.*

"The Navajo teach their children that every morning when the sun comes up, it's a brand-new sun. It's born each morning, it lives for the duration of one day, and in the evening it passes

Mrs. Sophie Kalmar, 11 years of age, 1931

on, never to return again. As soon as the children are old enough to understand, the adults take them out at dawn and they say, 'The sun has only one day. You must live this day in a good way, so that the sun won't have wasted precious time.' Acknowledging the preciousness of each day is a good way to live, a good way to reconnect with our basic joy."

❖

❖

Dr. James Mendola

*". . .we end each and every conversation with those three
little words, 'I love you.'"*

Dr. Waldinger, on my recent office visit, you asked that I
write to you about my philosophy of life. You also
requested that I insert any unique stories or events of my life. Of
course, I have had several happenings during my 61 years–most
of which are positive, but not especially unique.

Let me begin by saying that I am a proud product of a work-
ing-class family. My father, who is now 85, worked very hard in
the foundry of a steel mill in western Pennsylvania. My mother,
who is now 83, did not work outside the home. Her responsibility was to take care of my father, my sister (eight years younger
than I), and me. Needless to say, she did that very well and still
continues to do that today.

My father was a strong disciplinarian who would not hesitate
to use his strap on me during my younger years. I am sure that I
deserved it; however, I do not remember him ever using it on my
sister–probably because she did not deserve it.

As you can see, my parents had a strong influence on my life.
I was taught to have respect for others, especially for adults. In
addition to my parents, my high school and college coaches were
quite instrumental in my development. They, too, believed in
hard work and discipline.

Dr. James Mendola (far right) with sister, Donna, and his parents, 1986

Fortunately, I grew up liking to play ball–football, basketball and baseball. I was very competitive (still am today) and did fairly well in the sports arena. I guess athletics was my way of receiving attention and acceptance from my family and friends. I still have a scrapbook of my high school and college "clippings."

I was fortunate to get a football scholarship at a relatively small teachers college, which was located in a nearby community about a half-hour drive from my home. This college attracted many athletes from the coal mining areas that surrounded it. Many of us realized that this could be our way to get a college degree so that we would be able to teach and coach.

After graduating from college, I moved to Michigan to teach secondary school and coach. I soon began graduate work and received a master's degree, then an Educational Specialist degree, and eventually a doctorate degree. I did not get my doctorate until I was employed by the Detroit College of Business where I have been for nearly 30 years.

My philosophy in life is to work hard, be respectful of others, and good things will happen. So far, "good things" have happened and my life has been wonderful. I have a great family, good health (thanks to you), many wonderful friends, and a position that has enabled my family and me an opportunity to afford the finer things in life. In other words, I have been very lucky and quite appreciative for my quality of life. Also, I really find pleasure in giving back to others. This can be in the form of money, advice or material things. I guess I have realized that many people have given to me—so now it is my turn to act accordingly. I am a positive individual who sees the glass as being half full rather than half empty, and I look forward to getting up every morning to face the everyday challenges.

I attribute much of my success to my parents, who never graduated from high school. I always knew that they cared about my sister and me, even though they may not have said it. I am pleased to say that when I talk with my parents on the phone, we end each and every conversation with those three little words, "I love you." I feel very fortunate to still have my parents, especially because they are in fairly good health.

I only wish that other people could enjoy their lives as I enjoy mine. Some do, of course, and I am happy for them. This happiness is especially true now since I have had the extreme pleasure of being a grandfather for the past five years. As I said before—I am a very lucky person, and I know it and will always appreciate it.

Commentary:

Dr. James Mendola is one of the most positive people I have ever met. He exudes boundless energy and a "can do" spirit. I can imagine him working on the Apollo 13 Mission when the astronauts had no way to get home. Jim would say, "Failure is not an option."

There are times in medicine when I feel the workload is insurmountable. I lean on Jim's words and they buoy me each time. I hope they will lift you as well.

❖

Mrs. Eleanore Smith

*"First of all, I found out that anyone can accomplish
what he wants if the will and desire are there."*

The following is how I perceive my philosophy of life. I shall
attempt to tell you what I have discovered about life during
my 85 years. It will be necessary to tell you a little about my own
life in order to tell you what brought me to these evaluations.

First of all, I found out that anyone can accomplish what he
wants if the will and desire are there. As a young woman, I was
very sheltered and thought that life was only music and my
cello. However, at 30 years of age, I lost my husband in the war
and was left with a very small baby boy. It was at this time that I
found it was very important for me to bring up my child and
instill in him the things that were most important to me. This
meant no lying, being honest, no sneaking, no cheating and,
above all, having good morals.

Of course, I wanted the best I could give him, not necessarily
material things, but love and good values. Over the years I have
found that there is always some good in everyone if you stop to
look to for it. You do not always have to give material things, but
only give of yourself.

Trust your own instincts and don't let others try to influence
you. I worked hard at anything I could do to maintain a good life
for us. It was not always easy, and I'm sure I have made

Mrs. Eleanore Smith and son Erik (television news anchorman), 1948

many mistakes. But I have a wonderful son of whom I am very proud. Life is a great learning process. There may be a lot of bumps along the way, but friends and perseverance are priceless. Don't ever give up. Take what life offers you. Take it graciously and don't complain about the difficulties. Everyone has them!

Good friends are a wonderful gift, but you also must give of yourself and you will receive. I'm back again with my music and cello and I certainly enjoy sitting on the top of the ladder.

Commentary:

Mrs. Eleanore Smith's philosophy of life in the face of difficulties is very life-affirming. Mrs. Smith has shared her love of music with me. To this day, she is accomplishing her dreams. Mrs. Smith still performs in a community orchestra at the age of 85. She bestowed upon her son a great gift–her wisdom.

> Happy is the one who finds wisdom,
> the one who gains understanding;
>
> For its fruits are better than silver,
> its yield than fine gold.
>
> It is more precious than rubies;
> no treasure can match it.
>
> – Proverbs 8

Mrs. Mary Maynarich

*"Though my parents' knowledge of the English language
was limited, my mother's food reigned supreme."*

I have been married for 50 years and am a native of Michigan.
I attended Wayne State University and spent 32 years working in the business world. My mother and father immigrated to
this country when my mother was 19. I was born when she was
20, the eldest of three children. My parents were a gentle, loving,
caring couple and full of compassion for others.

Every Saturday morning my mother and I would pull my little red wagon to the Delray Market, about three miles away,
where I watched as she selected our fruits and vegetables. Back
home the cooking would begin. I can recall my mother rolling
out pastas, forming breads, and preparing all those other homey,
delicious dishes. It was at her side that I developed a love for
good food and cooking. She made the preparation of it seem like
a fun project, which it was.

During the holidays our large dining room table was laden
with wonderful food and crowded with relatives and our less
fortunate and elderly neighbors. Though my parents' knowledge
of the English language was limited, my mother's food reigned
supreme. I'm in my 70s and still cooking and baking—and loving
it! I call it my therapy!

Commentary:

As I was reading Mrs. Maynarich's wonderful statement, I thought about my daughter, Emily, and how much she also enjoys cooking. During an office visit, I had the opportunity to discuss Mrs. Maynarich's philosophy of life with her and told her about Emily's love of cooking. She subsequently wrote the following note for Emily:

"Doctor Waldinger: Here are a few of my favorite recipes. I'm always glad to help a young cook!"

Mrs. Maynarich, thank you for taking the time to share your knowledge of cooking with my daughter. Food is a universal language. I also want to thank my patients for the delicious homemade treats they often bring to the office. I have included one of Mrs. Maynarich's favorite recipes for everyone to enjoy.

Garden Vegetable Casserole

1 or 2 small eggplants
   (peeled)
1 small yellow squash
1 zucchini
1 sweet onion (quartered)
1 or 2 Yukon Gold potatoes
1 red sweet pepper or yellow
   pepper
1 carrot (sliced thin)

Slice all vegetables and toss with salt and pepper and olive oil mixed with balsamic vinegar. Place on sprayed cookie sheet and bake in 400-degree oven (preheated) for 20 to 25 minutes. (Use any vegetable leftover–such as sweet potato or turnip.) Sprinkle with Parmesan cheese (optional).

Mrs. Mary Maynarich (right) and her mother, Mrs. Jenny Orlandi, Phoenix, Arizona, August 1953

Mrs. Bette Mys

"Let's use the problems that come against us as opportunities to grow."

It's true I suffer from a chronic illness. However, my desire is to concentrate on living with the condition until a cure can be found. I am, like you, a pilgrim stumbling along the way, a common pilgrim with a common name: Bette. I wish I would be afforded healing and a cure. It would be wonderful for good health to return to my body so I could be the person I used to be. Being a loving wife to my husband, Don, and the best mother I can be to our daughters, Susan and Amy, is and will continue to be the most important thing in my life. Also, I've always tried to be a caring daughter, sister and friend.

My profession of teaching the blind and visually impaired afforded me much joy and pleasure. My students made each day so very special and I looked forward to spending time with all of them. I still recall one of my fifth graders who was more interested in using his slate and stylus as a musical-tapping instrument instead of as a tool for brailling and completing his work assignments. This young man's name is Stevie Wonder–someone who has made quite a name for himself in the music world. Stevie always has said that I was the strictest teacher that he ever had, but the best. I demanded a lot from my students and felt strongly that their academic potentials should always be challenged and met if possible.

At the age of 40, I was accepted into law school. At this time, my chronic illness became very debilitating. It was extremely difficult for me to keep on going. An internist told me that I was overextending myself and it was imperative that I give up law school, put my real estate license in escrow, and rest. However, I kept teaching until I was virtually forced to take an extended health leave. I have never given up my extended health leave status with the schools. I feel it is something that I will keep for as long as possible because I am confident it spurs me on in my search for better health, a cure, and the ability to someday return to teaching–my first career love.

My philosophy of life has been altered somewhat since the onset of my illness, but it remains basically the same. It revolves around love, faith, kindness, thoughtfulness, and generosity toward others. At present, it takes me longer to accomplish tasks and this often leads to much discouragement and disappointment on my part. It does, however, make me appreciate life so much more.

In the last few years my philosophy has also been challenged by personal circumstances. It was only through prayer, counseling and time that the situation has been resolved. Much peace within myself has occurred after I was asked by Dr. Waldinger to submit in writing some of my personal philosophical feelings toward life. Writing this statement has afforded me closure and the courage I desperately needed to move forward. I thank God every day for the changes that have occurred in my life and Dr. Waldinger for asking me to contribute my thoughts for his book. It was exactly what I needed at this time in my life and it has accomplished so much more than I ever expected. I will be forever grateful to him for allowing me to be a part of his meaningful publication.

I believe that what people need more than anything is God, their family and their friends' love for them personally. This to me is the foundation upon which living as a Christian is formed and this can be given to an individual only through the love of

God and prayer. God wants to have a personal relationship with you, but it is up to you to open up your heart to accept His love and understanding. People have a craving, and a longing and a desire in their hearts to be loved and cared about. The sun rises in the sky every day for you. When the rain comes in season, it rains for you. When the snow comes, it comes for you.

Sometimes, I thought that people could wear God out with their failures or problems, but I learned it is impossible to do that. In January of 1996, my world collapsed even more when Don suffered a massive coronary. Since that time, several other serious cardiac concerns have had to be addressed. Don lost more than one-third of his heart and has limited strength. Furthermore, the original angioplasty procedure failed and additional blockages were noted. I honestly do not think that God can be worn out or that He will ever stop loving you. Love is not something that God does, but it is who He is. He loves all people unconditionally regardless of their problems.

We all make mistakes and have shortcomings. I will always remember when one of my daughters, who was about 3 or 4 years old at the time, was watching me do my housework. She decided one day to help me and got a little bucket of water and a rag and went to the picture window on the front porch. She scrubbed the window really well, and got a few paper towels to wipe off the window. Of course, it was all streaky, smeary and soapy when she completed her job. She also used my best dusting cloth as her rag! She came up to me and told me that she had washed my window and did a good job. "I love you Mommy," she said. Yes, I thanked her for helping and I did clean up the mess, but did give her some encouragement later not to do that again. As I said before, God cleans up our messes, too. You must do the best that you know how to do. However, no one expects you to do something you are not able to do.

It is impossible to rise above the image of yourself that's in your head. My problem was that I didn't like being ill and still do not and spent a great deal of time trying to change myself. When I was quiet, others thought I was depressed. I did not want to bother anyone with my health concerns. Tremendous guilt was present but I found out that no matter how guilty you feel, that is not going to help you at all. You must learn to believe that God loves you even when you feel this way. Guilt only keeps you weighed down and discouraged to the point that you cannot be free. A person must say "no" to guilt. I have learned not to feel bad about talking to others about my concerns any longer. The first few times I did this were tough, but soon I got used to it and felt so much better.

I feel that you can express your feelings to people by just sharing love, faith, and trust with them. We must all strive at having more faith, but faith of the heart can be achieved only through loving relationships. A lot of people are trying to walk in faith, but they do not have these things in their heart. Faith will not work without love.

We usually go along just fine in faith. Then all of a sudden, something attacks us. The big stealer of faith is circumstances–those bad things that happen to all of us. A person who doesn't have much trouble believes that God loves you until the circumstances make it look like He doesn't. Then you lose your confidence and it is extremely difficult to move forward. You must at this time remember that you are special and you must start to act that way and it will begin to change your life in a positive way. Love will then spread. The love you have inside you will set you free from fear, and you will not be afraid to reach out to others with love.

> Nor height nor depth, nor anything else in all creation will be able to separate us from the love of God which is in Christ Jesus our Lord.
> – Romans 8:39

Do not expend all of your energy concentrating on yourself and getting your own needs met. Try to simply and quickly decide what you want and then move on to meet the needs of other people. Try also to use your strength to meet every need that comes before you. The needs of others should come first. It doesn't take anything to love somebody who loves you. There is no trust in that. But when you love the unlovable, you press on

Mrs. Bette Mys (left) and sister Jean, 1948

and keep loving them, and you keep loving them and keep loving them.

Also, don't be afraid to step out. Be determined to spread your love around. Start by just being friendly with others. Extend your hand to others and smile. Maybe you are that special person who nobody else can reach. Letting someone know that you care and love him will make you feel good. Just take that first step and see how much it will change your life forever.

Let's use the problems that come against us as opportunities to grow. Never forget about your strong faith. If you experience love, you will be smiling all the time. Energy and strength come from loving others. Furthermore, something that Don and I have always had during extremely difficult times is a positive attitude and we are always confident that healthier and happier times are just around the corner. We also believe that God would not bestow upon us more that we could bear–although at times we did have to question God and felt we could not handle one more hardship. But, to our surprise, we knew our faith in God, the love of family and friends, and the kind and thoughtful ways of our doctors would get us through even the toughest of times. God bless you all and thank you for your caring ways. We will always hold a special place in our hearts for each and every one of you.

Is there a light at the end of the tunnel? We seem to think so even though that light may just be a glimmer at times and not that bright and shining beam that we desire to see. We have learned that hope and prayer will make it in life no matter what obstacles we might encounter along the way. Health problems are unavoidable but can be faced and challenged with the proper support team. Our life has been blessed with the kindness and caring of family, friends and the best physicians. We are, and have been, truly fortunate to have these special individuals touch our lives so deeply and profoundly. Someone to talk to in time of need is so important and can make an unforgettable impact on a person's life.

Commentary:

Several years ago, Mrs. Bette Mys offered to be a volunteer in my office. She said that due to her chronic illness she was limited but would help in any way she could. Despite her medical limitations, she wanted to help. I was very touched by her thoughtfulness and generosity. Because there was adequate staffing for my clerical needs, I told Bette her help in the office was not necessary at that time. She responded that I should let her know if circumstances should change. Over the years, Bette continued to remind me of her desire to volunteer in the office.

When I decided to write *The Wisdom of Life Through My Patients*, I asked Bette if she would contribute her philosophy. Her wisdom touches us all and helps us in our daily lives. Bette also offered to help me with editorial assistance. There have been so many wonderful things that have occurred in the process of writing this book; the growth of our friendship is one and this has had an unforgettable impact on my life.

I used to have lunch with Dr. Ulrich the first five years of my practice. The time spent with him was very precious. Fourteen years later, I was joined again at lunchtime by a very special friend, Mrs. Bette Mys. The time spent with Bette has been precious to me as well.

Mrs. Betty Coogan

"A simple toy can bring you a lot of fun and love."

Since the death of my husband from lung cancer almost three years ago, I've had a lot of time to think and reflect on my life. There have been many lonely hours with nothing more to do than think and remember and get through the grieving.

I have been blessed with three sons and daughters-in-law, seven grandchildren, four sisters and two brothers. Also many, many nieces and nephews. They have been very kind and helpful to me in many ways.

There is one favorite nephew who stands out among them, named Dave. He too has suffered greatly and has had a lot of sorrow in his young life. When he comes over to visit me, we find ourselves sitting in the kitchen having coffee and doing a lot of talking and soul-searching about the family, feelings and memories. Somehow he has been a mentor to me. For a young man he has a lot of common sense and wisdom. He gave me the courage to go on with my life and do the things I want to do and I love him for that.

One day I was talking to Dave about my childhood. I remembered as a small girl looking forward to Christmas. It was during the Depression years and our family was on welfare like so many others. There were no gifts because we had no money. I'm sure

Mrs. Coogan, on swing, 1939

my parents felt terrible but there was nothing they could do. At
that time there were 11 children–four brothers and six sisters. I
was the youngest. My parents had emigrated from Italy in 1910.
They both came from poor families so hard times were nothing
new to them.

Christmas morning came and to our surprise the Goodfellows
came to our house and brought each of us a gift. Mine was a
beautiful, colorful rubber ball. I was so happy with that ball! It
brought me much joy, love and happiness. I have never forgotten
that Christmas!

I told Dave that is why I always purchased my children and
grandchildren rubber balls to play with–large, small and colorful ones. I would spend many hours playing games with them

and enjoying their laughter. A simple toy can bring you a lot of fun and love.

When I was through talking, Dave said to me, "Aunt Betty, what a beautiful story you just told me about your life. Without even being aware, you were sharing and giving the gift of love to your children and grandchildren because that is what that rubber ball did for you on that Christmas morning." He was so right! I never saw it so clearly before. It was another one of moments of our sharing our feelings that really help me to grow and discover myself as the person I really am with a lot of love to give my family.

Now that I am older, I still love seeing children play ball. Whenever I go shopping and see colored balls in the stores, I can't help but smile. I remember how the gift of love, through a simple rubber ball, brought so much happiness to one little girl on that Christmas Day so long ago. It continues to extend the gift of love to me and my family today.

Commentary:

To My Children, Jason and Emily:

Mrs. Coogan's story reminds me of all the balls that we have thrown, caught, hit, tossed and kicked. Those sporting activities included tennis, basketball, soccer, baseball, ping-pong and golf. I served as your coach for four of these sports. You introduced me to golf. In every instance we shared good times and love. As we continue to play sports throughout our lives, we will be reminded of Mrs. Coogan's wonderful philosophy. Remember her thoughts when you play with your children.

---❖---

Mrs. Elizabeth Leach

*"What then would I tell my grandson and granddaughter
if they were to say to me today, 'Grandma, tell us about
your life.'"*

I believe that there is a power greater than myself always
available to me. I believe that within each of us is a God-
given potential to be developed. My strength comes from my
steadfast faith that I am never really alone and that the spirit of
God within me will give me the strength and guidance to meet
and to withstand whatever comes to me in life.

This all sounds like a very easy and simple philosophy.
However, to actually live by this belief is not always easy. Fears,
doubts, anger, insecurities, disappointments, illnesses and losses
of many kinds have confronted me and made it a challenge to
stay on track to develop my potential to the fullest and to practice the faith I profess.

In my many years of life there have been wonderful and
happy times with many advantages and opportunities. There
also have been disadvantages and lonely and depressing times.
What then would I tell my grandson and granddaughter if they
were to say to me today, "Grandma, tell us about your life." The
first things that would come to me would not be the sad parts of
my life. Rather, I would probably tell them of how I grew up on a
farm—loving, laughing and "fighting" with my three brothers. I
entertained myself walking rail fences, climbing in haymows,

and playing barefoot in the river that ran through the back of our farm. Stories of how we would be snowed in for several days in the winter would also be included. This gave us a real opportunity for family togetherness. I still have fond memories of the taffy, fudge and popcorn being made during these times and I remember the real happiness of looking up the road and seeing a snowplow coming to free us.

Among these stories, it must not be forgotten that there were always chores around the farm to be done and each family member had definite responsibilities. Somehow, I would want my grandchildren to know how the activities at the little church in the village played an all-important part of the person I am today. One of the most significant stories would include my loving, hardworking, creative and devoted parents who gave me support during good times, lonely and uncertain times and also during the times I would want to try my wings and do new things.

This example stands out in my memory. I very much wanted to play in the high school band. However, we could not afford to buy an instrument. My mother came up with the idea that she would give me 100 baby chicks to care for during the summer. In the fall, I sold the grown chickens and proudly bought a new clarinet. Playing in the high school band gave me a feeling of fulfillment and self-worth.

I may include in my stories the fact that my leg was in a cast and brace during the ages of 3 to 7. I still remember when, at the end of the four years, the doctor had me walk across the room. When he saw that my leg was straightened and healed, he said to me, "God has performed a miracle." That statement from the doctor has had an influence on how I've tried very hard to always develop my potential to the fullest.

I would hope that from these stories, lessons would be learned. These would include the lessons of the importance of being creative in the environment in which we find ourselves, by seeking out interesting things to do, and not always having to depend on others to entertain us. Also, it is important to know how happiness can come from doing simple things. I would stress the importance of belonging and of helping others and the importance of knowing what is expected of us by having responsibilities and chores to do. Moreover, I would include the lesson of the significance of making commitments to oneself and to others and how all these things work together to give us a good self-image and a feeling of self-worth.

Mrs. Elizabeth Leach, 1997

Random Closing Thoughts

The clouds in your life can make beautiful sunsets.

Know yourself and be true to yourself.

Learn from your experiences–both good experiences and not so good ones.

Don't expect other people to please you all the time.

Don't feel that you always have to please other people all the time.

It is impossible to make everyone like you all the time.

Don't depend on other people for your complete happiness. We should not give others the burden of making us happy. Develop deep inner resources upon which you can always depend.

I try to remember that real happiness can come from knowing who we are. I believe to know myself and understand what kind of a person I really am and knowing what kind of a person I want to be are imperative in developing my potential to the fullest. To develop your potential is an ongoing process.

Try to learn something useful from all experiences.

Use blame and criticism from others as stepping stones to add still another dimension to your philosophy of life.

Keeping the right attitude is of utmost importance in living a happy and fulfilled life. Our attitude toward ourselves, toward others, and our attitude toward situations is very important. Actually, almost any problem in life can be made easier to face and solve by having a positive yet realistic attitude toward it.

In closing, I would like to say that people need the love and fellowship of other people. God works through us to make this world a better place.

Commentary:

In my early years of practice, Mrs. Floria Mader invited me to have tea at her home. I always visited her on Fridays at the end of my day. She was approaching 90 years of age at that time. Mrs. Mader has since passed away.

I once talked with Mrs. Leach in the office about her philosophy of life and how she reminded me of Mrs. Mader even though she is much younger. We both agreed we should have tea together at her home at the conclusion of my book. Mrs. Leach, I am looking forward to tea and learning more about the wisdom you have shared with us. Your thoughts will always encourage me to believe in myself and try new things.

Mr. Herbert Haslam

"To me, one of the most satisfying aspects of police work was being of assistance to people, always trying to be fair and just."

I was born in Ontario, Canada, of an English father and Welsh mother. We immigrated to the United States and I attended schools in Detroit, Michigan. I left school before finishing due to a move from Detroit to an area that had no high school. I later obtained my high school diploma.

I worked in an auto plant from 1939 until 1943 when I enlisted in the U.S. Navy Seabees construction battalions, serving most of the time in the southwest Pacific. Most of this overseas duty I spent as a welder in heavy equipment repair. I also served and lived on a floating dry dock while it was assembled and lived aboard the *U.S.S. Houston* for a month doing damage repair after it suffered two torpedo hits in the Philippine invasion.

Upon returning to civilian life, I returned to my job in the auto plant until I was accepted as an officer on the police force in Wayne, Michigan, in 1947. At about the same time I learned to fly, eventually accumulating approximately 250 hours of flying time including aerobatics. I married Helen, a WWII Army nurse at that time, and we have three fine children. I believe my desire to become a police officer may have been influenced by two Detroit officers I became acquainted with while I was a safety patrol boy in elementary school. Mr. Stevens and Mr. Hill both happened to be black, which was unusual at that time even in Detroit. I admired both of them and their attitudes toward their chosen profession.

As an officer in a small department, I performed various duties–patrol, motorcycle duty, and investigative–rising through the ranks to captain. As captain, I was second in command in a department consisting of 39 sworn officers and 18 civilians.

I had numerous interesting experiences as an officer and distinguished myself on different occasions. I assisted in the apprehension of a suspect who was later proven to have killed a gas station attendant in New Jersey and two police officers in Virginia. The next night he fled from my partner and me, resulting in an accident in which he killed yet another man.

On another occasion, while off duty and alone, I apprehended four subjects for armed robbery. There were also arrests for breaking and entering, car theft, assaults, and numerous disorderly persons.

I remember a call to a home where a somewhat buxom woman had her breast caught in a wringer (actually, in the wringer gear case). After we released her and determined that she was not seriously injured, this became humorous to both her and us.

I have had my neck gouged by an unruly woman's fingernails, covering my white uniform shirt with blood, causing some concern to my wife when I went home to change. I wrestled a woman off of a parking meter and arrested another woman who cut a man's throat (he recovered). I also wrestled another woman around the street (she was a tough factory worker). Along the way I adopted a rule of thumb: 10 unruly men equal one unruly woman.

I remember going to deliver a "death message." The French poodle at the house seemed to sense that something was wrong, beginning to wail incessantly, almost as if it were crying!

I only shot at one subject. He was driving a reported stolen car. I was greatly relieved when I missed, because it was determined to be his grandmother's car.

I attended numerous police-related schools during my tenure, accumulating a few college credits.

To me, one of the most satisfying aspects of police work was being of assistance to people, always trying to be fair and just. I retired with 32 years of service. Throughout my life, I believe some of the most desirable attributes are: honesty, integrity and loyalty.

Capt. Herbert Haslam, Wayne Police Department, 1977

Commentary:

Mr. Herbert Haslam has always demonstrated the attributes he holds most dear: honesty, integrity and loyalty. I have known Mr. Haslam and his wife since I started my practice in Dearborn. Although we have talked many times, I never knew that he dedicated his life to law enforcement. What I find most interesting is the positive effect two Detroit policemen had on an elementary school patrol boy.

It is the responsibility of every adult, and physicians in particular, to recognize the potential influence we have on others. This impact can have a greater effect on children and young adults as they form their beliefs and make career decisions.

The world is changed by one person taking an interest or being a role model for another. The two Detroit policemen were probably unaware that they helped to shape Mr. Haslam's life.

❖

Mrs. Margaret Reilly

"My Uncle Lee. . .reminds me of Dr. Ulrich; both were tall, handsome, kind and gentle. Every time Uncle Lee and I parted, he said, 'Sugar, if you need anything at all, just call me.' Dr. Ulrich's parting words were, 'Bless you.'"

It is important that I start these remarks by saying that my sister and I are a mixture of Northern "Yankee" (so called by my mother's family) and a soft, gentle Southern woman. My father was born into a prominent, prosperous Michigan farm family, who enjoyed a warm, wonderful life with an abiding faith in God and in education. His parents' dream for their three sons was that some day they would attend college and earn engineering degrees. When my dad was 8 years old, his mother died, and then four years later, his father was killed in a car accident. Eventually the inheritance disappeared and the boys were placed in a Chicago orphanage. The youngest boy stayed in the institution and graduated from high school, the middle boy ran away, and the oldest boy, my dad, stayed until sometime during high school and then returned to Michigan to fish and to be with his brother.

When dad was in his early 20s, he went to Ford Motor Company's Rouge manufacturing complex in search of a job. At 5:00 in the morning applicants formed a line outside the employment office. After the candidates were chosen for the jobs that day, a Ford personnel employee approached dad and said, "If you had not been standing with your hands in your pockets, you would have gotten a job today." Needless to say, at 5:00 the next morning dad was back in line, standing with his arms straight down at his sides. He was hired that day and worked at Ford Motor Company for 43 years. It was not uncommon for Henry Ford to look over dad's shoulders watching him work. Dad attended Henry Ford Trade School, worked on experimental projects, such as automatic transmissions, and received Ford Motor Company's highest monetary award for the invention (one among a number of others he was too humble to claim) of cost-saving machinery. Dad was a very bright, dedicated,

Mrs. Margaret Reilly and dad, 1943

loyal employee, often working seven days a week for months on end, absent one day for the birth of a daughter (my sister) and late one morning because of car trouble. Without question, dad possessed exemplary work ethics, a product of the Great Depression that impressed upon him a set of rules for the rest of his life, ethics conferred upon his daughters. No doubt about it.

Dad believed education guaranteed a means to earn a decent living and a way to keep you out of long employment lines. Education is exactly what he wanted for his daughters: My sister graduated from a California university with a Bachelor of Science in Business and subsequently earned her C.P.A. She began her professional career as the first woman auditor in Los Angeles for Arthur Andersen and Company, one of the largest accounting firms in the world. She went on to become vice president of finance for a southern California hospital and medical center. I earned a Bachelor of Science and a Master of Arts and Business and taught in secondary schools for over 30 years.

I am proud to report that, from both sides of the family, we have 17 first cousins, 11 of whom are college graduates—accountants, engineers, lawyers, teachers, a world-class scientist, a doctor, a nurse and a minister. Education was stressed by our parents for their children to turn out so successfully, and the next generation is continuing the tradition even better.

My husband earned degrees—bachelor's through doctorate—from four Michigan universities. Dad was in his glory sitting in Hill Auditorium at the University of Michigan watching his son-in-law receive his doctorate. This experience was beyond his dreams.

Mom was a soft, gentle, kind Southern lady from Tennessee, reared in an area in which church was the center of the community, surrounded by farms of family and friends. Mom had five brothers and one sister, a very tightly knit group of family members who dearly loved each other and remained close throughout their lifetimes. When mom was about 19, she was invited to Detroit to visit her brother, Lee, who had left the farm to seek work. It was at this time that mom met dad before returning to Tennessee, only to receive shortly thereafter a diamond engagement ring via U.S. mail. She accepted. The next time the young couple saw each other was on the occasion when dad traveled to Tennessee to marry mom. Mom was a hard-working mother at home, in the church, and at jobs outside our home. These jobs provided her daughters such things as spending money in college or a new dress for a party, or a new hat for mom. The last job mom had was at American Motors in the private dining room of George Rommey, who became governor of Michigan.

When dad died at 90 years of age, he and mom had been married for 65 years. Mom also lived to 90 years as well.

My Uncle Lee, referred to above, reminds me of Dr. Ulrich; both were tall, handsome, kind and gentle. Every time Uncle Lee and I parted, he said, "Sugar, if you need anything at all, just call me." Dr. Ulrich's parting words were, "Bless you."

These men spent their lives helping people—friends and strangers alike—splendid examples of manhood, gentlemen.

My mirror reflects a precious family and friends: hardworking, honest, self-sufficient, unassuming. These loved ones honored family life, each other, and their friends faithfully throughout their lives. We always had time to help neighbors, those in need, and especially those who were ill. We were simple, God-loving people.

Mrs. Reilly's Uncle Al, Uncle Earl and father, 1920

Dr. Bernard Reilly

"LOVE SERVES"

When one considers what the word "professional" means in the real world of business, industry, medicine or education–that is, in the daily lives of people who depend upon trust in a reciprocal relationship–Drs. Ulrich and Waldinger shine as symbols of warmth, competence and dedication to the sacredness of human life with an abiding faith in the Almighty. LOVE SERVES.

I remember Sandy Ulrich, who was a student in a 10th grade English class I was teaching at Dearborn High School, a sparkling young lady, full of youthful enthusiasm, and ready to make a most positive contribution when called upon to do so. Sandy's parents instilled in her their philosophy: LOVE SERVES.

Many of us foster this philosophy in our lives and seek to maintain the values nurtured in us so that the alien forces of the world remain in check. That's partly why I have evolved as a professor of English, contending with the daily challenges of motivating students to grow and to succeed in maximizing their own reading and writing proficiencies. Educators witness the rewards of minds ignited by the power of learning. LOVE SERVES.

A graduate classmate said to me one time, "Why are you going into teaching? Why are you wasting your energies working with students when with your credentials you could be so much more?" Strangely enough, we were both in the same program seeking our Doctorates in English Language and Literature with the ultimate objective of teaching in the community college. I was speechless at these questions; dumbfounded that our goals were so different when I expected we both had similar ambitions, not dissimilar ones. On another occasion an "innocent" student remarked, "You're too good to be working with these students." But LOVE SERVES.

Dr. Bernard Reilly receiving his Doctorate in English Language and Literature, University of Michigan, December 1973

It is a blessing when we recognize our role in the workplace allows us to earn our way and concomitantly contribute to the well-being of the world in which we live. That's what the Ulriches, the Waldingers, and the Reillys, et al–God willing–are about. LOVE SERVES.

Commentary:

I am very grateful for all that Dr. and Mrs. Reilly have shared with me. A special thank you to Mrs. Reilly for the delicious muffins she often brought to my office. In the practice of medicine, the love that you give your patients is always returned. As Dr. Reilly so eloquently writes, "Love serves."

❖

❖

Mrs. Geraldine Mattox

"Grandma Lovejoy was a remarkable lady. She was the postmaster of the town for 28 years."

I was born March 17, 1902, in the home of my grandmother, Amanda Lovejoy. My parents were Frank and Pearl Beatty. They lived to celebrate 50 years of marriage.

Grandma Lovejoy was a remarkable lady. She was the postmaster of the town for 28 years. She was a teacher of organ music and wrote for the village newspaper. She also did watercolor painting and served on the jury in circuit and federal courts. She was a big influence in my life.

When I was 10 years old, my grandmother took me to a rented cottage on Lake Huron. While there, she purchased the lot next door and the following year had a three-bedroom cottage built. It was enjoyed by the family for many years. I spent my summer vacations there until I married. I was called a bookworm when in school. I loved to study and read. When I was 12 years old, my parents gave me a desk for my room so I wouldn't be bothered by my two younger sisters and a brother. In high school I decided to be a librarian, and I had one year of community college. Then my father lost his job and I thought I had better get a job to help out at home.

I was a dental assistant for four years for four dentists. I married John D. Howells in 1926. He was a wood patternmaker for

General Motors. He was a very kind and generous man. We were married 52 years. We had two sons, David and Paul. David died of cancer at age 55. Paul is still living but has emphysema, so I don't see much of him. I was a widow for four years when I met Edward Mattox at a seniors meeting. I had no intention of marrying again, but I did want to travel. Edward talked a lot about traveling. We both bought tickets for the World's Fair in Tennessee. We got aquainted there and I married him in 1980. I was 78 years old. We had a good 14-1/2 years of marriage before he passed away.

I feel very fortunate to be able to stay in my apartment. I have a jewel of a cleaning lady and get Home-Delivered Meals five days a week. Edward's oldest son is a blessing to me. He calls me every day and takes me to some of my doctor appointments.

I have been a member of Littlefield Presbyterian Church for 52 years. I was in the first Deacons class and when I was ordained, I felt the hand of the Lord on my shoulder and He has guided me ever since. I have many friends at Littlefield Presbyterian Church. Two of them are volunteers for FISH. They help me with transportation. Edward asked his son, Edsel, to look after me. He was with his father the day before he died. I had a good life with Edward. Being in Florida away from the cold has helped me to live to my age. I am very thankful for my many blessings.

Commentary:

Mrs. Geraldine Mattox is a special lady and one of my oldest patients. Her energy and intelligence are amazing.

Because she enjoys such longevity, I always ask Mrs. Mattox at each office visit what she has eaten that day. She is very precise about her meals and especially the portions that she eats. Mrs. Mattox is always willing to share her thoughts about good nutrition and kind enough to give me a detailed menu for the day. In his book, *The 22 Non-Negotiable Laws of Wellness*, Greg Anderson talks about the importance of "The Law of

Nutritional Frugality." Mrs. Mattox is a living example of this law.

Mrs. Mattox, you write about your Grandma Lovejoy and the big influence she had on your life. I want you to know that you have had a big impact on me and upon my entire office staff.

Edward and Geraldine Mattox, 1982

❖

Dr. Robert Young

Commentary:

The next philosophy of life statement is a trilogy with universal meaning. Dr. Young's "To Jackie on Time at Twelve" is a poignant letter to his granddaughter. Dr. Young provides a loving foundation for the guidance and wisdom needed at a time of great change in children's lives. However, the letter can help anyone at any age. It has helped me.

The section entitled "Relationships between Perceived Love and Perceived Expectations in Adolescents" provides novel and important insight for parents like Marcy and me who are currently raising adolescent children. It serves as a guide to instill the values espoused by Dr. Young. Parents can use it as a blueprint for the transition from adolescence to successful adulthood.

Dr. Young's last segment is "Final Words." It is a poem that he has written to be read at his memorial service. The poem is a reflection of his wonderful philosophy of life. His words always bring me back to the purpose of my book—to seek wisdom from people in our lives.

To Jackie on Time at Twelve
by Dr. Robert Young

On a cold, snowy day in December of 1980, you slipped out of your mother's womb and into this thing man calls time.

You brought with you no material possessions: no hat, no shoes, no blanket, no stocks or bonds.

Greater, however, than all the world's material possessions, you came in a body, with no parts needing to be recalled: a body in which you could travel through what man calls time.

Twelve years have passed since that snowy day, and you are now at the age where your journey through time will be guided more and more by you and less and less by mom and dad.

Some of your friends will think this means more freedom and eventually to be free at last, but always remember that you are never really free because you will always be responsible for the decisions you are free to make.

To make good decisions is often a difficult process, especially during the teens when the development of one's body outpaces the development of one's mind.

This body clock and mind clock inside each of us get out of sync for a short period early in our lives, but each of us must do our best to make good decisions in spite of this challenge.

Life, this passage through time, can often be tough and challenging but yet a beautiful and rewarding experience, or it can often be tough and challenging and a very depressing experience.

The decisions you make along the way will determine the kind of experience you will have in this thing called time, so strive to make good decisions.

You will not always make the "right" decision but remember two things: You should always learn from your mistakes and making a mistake would never change the love we have for you.

Opal and Robert Young with grandchildren, Ryan and Jacklyn, 1989

Growing up may be the most difficult thing you ever have to do, and the biggest mistake you can make is to be in a hurry.

When you are 16 make decisions of a 16-year-old and not the decisions of a 20-year-old as so many young people do.

Getting a good education through college is the minimum foundation you will need for the challenges to be faced in your journey through time.

Know always that you have been loved from the moment you arrived, but know also that love does not dictate that those who love each other must always agree.

Finally, you need to know that this thing called time is nothing more than the movement of matter through space; the movement of the earth around the sun.

You need also to know that this movement has been going on for eons and many before you have made the journey on which you have embarked.

At the end of this journey, we all depart with no material possessions, and we leave behind the body which inserted us into time, a body recalled only once.

Remember always that your mom, your dad, your brother, and your grandparents love you and want only the very best for you in your journey through this thing man calls time.

Your Bubba

Relationship between Perceived Love and Perceived Expectations in Adolescents

by Dr. Robert Young

In the spring of 1998 at an appointment with Dr. Waldinger, he asked me about the things that have made a difference in my life. As I reflected on this question, there were three things which entered my mind. Three times in my life I had felt a compelling drive to put some thoughts on paper. At that point in life two had been accomplished and one had not.

The first was a letter which I presented to my granddaughter on her 12th birthday. After having spent a lifetime working with young people, I felt that I recognized some areas in her life which needed shoring up. The letter, which is reproduced here, is as it was originally written. The second time was the poem which has been written to be read at my memorial service.

The third, which is currently being written as I write this, deals with a theory that I developed early in my school administrative career. It guided me in my dealing with high school and junior high school youth as I worked with them endeavoring to get them to apply themselves to the fullest extent possible. I trust that what I have written will expand your thinking and be of benefit to you.

In October 1967, at the age of 39 and with 9-1/2 years' teaching experience, I was appointed to the position of assistant principal at an urban high school. Prior to that I had grown up in a very loving home, survived two years in the U.S. Navy, spent two years working in a factory, and attended college. As I look back on this now at the age of 70, even though I was middle-aged in 1967, I had lived a rather sheltered life.

The position of assistant principal presented daily challenges so severe that for the first six months I left work every day with a severe headache. In addition to the headaches, I was learning much about the wide range of relationships which exist between adults (parents and teachers) and high school age youth.

One of the first insights I developed was that young people are very resilient to change, but one thing which the vast majority could not handle was the breakup of the family. Parents could move the family from house to house, from city to city, and from state to state, but tear apart the family and you have torn apart the only world the child knows and cares about. Over the years I developed great respect for the couples who could put aside their personal differences and bite their lip until the children in the family were old enough to have left home before a breakup occurred in the family. Selfishness on the part of too many adults has left youth with nothing to hold on to and nothing to care about. Far too many young adults take too lightly the responsibility given them by our Supreme Being when they bring babies into this world.

And now the compelling theory which guided me in my many years as a school administrator. This theory was probably developed during the first three or four years I worked as a high school assistant principal. It was during this period that I first began to recognize the vast differences which existed in the relationships between parents and their children or teachers and their students. Before I go further, I want to state that this theory holds true to any adult who has a relationship with a young person, whether as a parent, grandparent, teacher, minister, or as a leader of a youth group.

Young people, even babies, have an innate ability to make judgments about their relationships with adults. They may not have accumulated in their brain the history of the human race, but they do have the ability to make a judgment regarding how little or how greatly an adult cares for them as a human being. The amount of caring that is displayed by the adult does not translate one-on-one to the caring perceived by the youth. And, it is the amount of caring perceived by the youth that is key, and the adult in this relationship must be able to relatively gauge this perception.

The second factor in this theory is the expectations, which the adult can reasonably expect the young person to make a concerted effort to achieve. The greater the youth's perceived love and concern flowing from the adult to the young person, the greater can be the expectations placed on the young person. It is the responsibility of the adult to perceive and keep in balance in the mind of the young person the relationship between the perceived love and concern and the perceived expectations of the adult. If the perceived love and concern are great then the expectations can be great, but if the perceived love and concern are low then the expectations should also be low. Get these two factors out of balance in the mind of the young person and problems arise.

To illustrate the above point, consider for a moment a young person who perceives great love and concern flowing from the adult to the youth but perceived expectations are very low. All too frequently this situation produces a young person we call "spoiled." Spoiled because the only expectation placed on the young person is to do his/her own thing and ask for what is wanted. Good grades or chores around the house are not expected. The attitude developed in the mind of the young person is that I am so good that I can do whatever I please and get away with it.

Consider also the young person who perceives very little love and concern flowing from the adult, but yet the perceived expectations placed on the young person are very great. The relation on the part of the young person is rebellion–why should I do all this work for you–you do not care anything about me. Child abuse frequently comes from homes where the parents want their children to be good and do the right thing, but the parents do not have the ability to convey a message of love and concern for the child.

Through my 25 years as a school administrator, my years as a parent and grandparent, and as an observant adult, I believe that an adult who can accurately read these perceived relationships in the mind of a young person can significantly and predictably guide the maturation and development of the young person.

Dr. Robert Young, school administrator

Final Words
by Dr. Robert Young

Mourn not for me that life is done;
My final adventure has just begun.
Reflect now on the life we've had;
It brought us both the good and bad.

Remember not the harder days,
But rather share our common ways.
Seek out today my living kin, and
Let them know just where we've been.

Speak out about the fun we had, and
Let them know that death's not sad.

Three goals were set to live each day;
I selfishly wanted my final pay.
To live my life as God saw fit,
I sought to give that extra bit.

To make the world a better place,
Has brought a smile to the human face.
To hear the laughter in your voice,
Was for me a daily choice.

To make you laugh has been one call;
It's your turn now to field the ball.

Thanks much, and look forward.
Look back only to learn.

Your friend,
Bob

Mrs. Helen Long

*"My approach to life is deeply rooted in my faith in God,
acknowledging that God may not come when I call Him,
but knowing that God will always show up on time!"*

My parents were Harry and Gladys Hutchinson of Detroit,
Michigan. I was the fifth of an eventual 12 children, having one older sister and three older brothers. We were poor, but
we didn't realize it. It was the time of the Great Depression and
we were in the same predicament as many of our neighbors. My
father was an auto mechanic and my mother a homemaker. My
mother "ruled the roost" and my father, a softie, was the peace-
maker. To supplement our table, we grew and canned our own
fruits and vegetables. Our home was always spotless and our
clothes were always clean. This despite the fact that we did not
have a washing machine and therefore used a washboard and
hung our clothes on a line out of doors. I can remember my
mother saying over and over again, "You only have one set of
clothes; keep them clean!" and that we did. Even now, some 71
years and many sets of clothes later, I still adhere to her philosophy. Another defining character trait of mine which may be
traced to the words of my mother is to be "friendly, but to keep
your distance."

In addition to family and home, there was a high priority
placed on going to church and going to school. Church was and
still is an important part of my life. Growing up, going to school

was a given. I gladly went there to learn. Reading was my best subject. When I was young, I would often take a flashlight to bed and read while under the covers, late into the night. Today you will seldom find me without a book in hand. Sometimes I read two to three books simultaneously, with where I am in the house determining which book I pick up and continue reading. As it was when I was a child, reading is my way of escaping, escaping to eras long past.

As the years went by, our family grew. Thank God, the economy also grew. As finances improved, so did our lives. We eventually moved into a home with a large yard, fruit trees, an enclosed back porch and enough room to comfortably house all of us. As I look back on this period of my life, I can remember coming home from church on a Sunday to find daddy making ice cream, churning it on that back porch and each of us kids jockeying to be allowed to lick the freshly made confection from the dasher. Even now when I close my eyes, I can still see this scene as clearly as if it were yesterday.

In 1945, I graduated from high school and began working as an employee of the city of Detroit. In 1950, I married John T. Long Jr., the love of my life. We were blessed with four children—one daughter, Michelle Yvette (1952) and three sons: John Thomas III (1955), Kevin Hutchinson (1959) and Michael Edward (1965). Michelle lives in Houston, Texas, with her attorney husband Andrew (McGhee). They are parents to two sons, Mari and Zachary. The Reverend John T. Long III lives in Daytona Beach, Florida, along with his wife, Maria, a corporate consultant, and their son, John IV. Their daughter, Nicole, is a sophomore at Wayne State University, Detroit. Kevin lives in Fort Worth, Texas, with his wife, Francesca, a student, and their three sons: Timar, a sophomore at the University of Texas North, Kevin, and Jonathan. Michael and his wife, Courtney, still live in Detroit with their three daughters: Taja, Kyla and Kyra.

In January 1985, my husband of 35 years suffered a fatal heart attack. I know that he is still watching over us and that he is as proud as I am of what each of our children has achieved. Our children are all married, all working, and are all providing a good foundation for their own children.

John and Helen Long, wedding day, 1950

My mother-in-law, who passed away in August 1984, always used to say, "I may not have monetary wealth, but I am the richest woman in the world. I have the love of my grandchildren." I too feel the same, exact way. She taught me so much which has helped to sustain me. I have often said, "If I can be half the mother-in-law to my children's spouses that she was to me, they will have nothing to worry about." Daisy, you were the greatest!

In the 1980s, after suffering several years with a chronic and life-altering skin condition, I met the young Dr. Thomas Waldinger during one of my many stays at the University of Michigan Hospital, Ann Arbor, Michigan. I found his bedside manner like that portrayed by doctors in the movies, only he was not acting out a role. He was a medical resident, studying to specialize in dermatology. We were doctor and patient and, over the succeeding years, we have become friends. My medical condition–prurigo nodularis–is indigenous to women of color or darker skin. I had given up all hope of wearing short pants and short-sleeved shirts ever again, but thanks to the unceasing efforts and medical care of Dr. Waldinger, my skin has cleared to the point that I can.

Once Dr. Waldinger submitted a paper to a dermatology journal concerning my condition and his conclusions. Dr. Waldinger is now in private practice and I see him on a scheduled basis. I am happy to say that under his care I have continued to improve. I am forever indebted to Dr. Waldinger for all that he has been able to accomplish in treating my condition. He is both a gentle man in temperament and a gentleman in character.

My approach to life is deeply rooted in my faith in God, acknowledging that God may not come when I call Him, but knowing that God will always show up on time! I know that without God I cannot do anything and that my very life and the lives of those whom I love are forever in His hands. I rise every morning with a prayer of thanksgiving for my life. Regardless of the outside conditions, whether rain, sunshine or snow, I thank God every day for every day.

My daily prayer is that my children and their children will recognize the treatment of my condition as a blessing from God and that they will give Him all the praise and glory, for He and He alone is worthy to be praised. Amen.

Commentary:

In December of 1984, Dr. Ulrich and I signed an agreement in which I would purchase his practice and building in Dearborn, Michigan. The practice was approximately 35 minutes from where I completed my dermatology residency. Although many of the patients I had cared for lived closer to the new office, I never discussed the upcoming move with them. This was done out of respect for the University of Michigan Department of Dermatology.

However, I had formed close relationships with many patients and knew that I would miss them when I started my own private practice in July. Mrs. Helen Long was one of these patients. I remember when I met Mrs. Long and the sincere desire that I had to improve or cure her chronic dermatological condition. I reviewed all of the therapeutic modalities that Mrs. Long had received and implemented a new therapy. This resulted in a publication in the *Archives of Dermatology*. I never had the chance during my residency to tell Mrs. Long that my paper had been accepted for publication.

Several years after I started my practice in Dearborn, Mrs. Long located me and scheduled an appointment. It was special to see her again. She includes in her statement of philosophy that, "My daily prayer is that my children and their children will recognize the treatment of my condition as a blessing from God and that they will give Him all the praise and glory, for He and He alone is worthy to be praised. Amen."

I am thankful for the opportunity to know Mrs. Helen Long. Her friendship and grace have meant so much to me.

❖

Mrs. Bernice Button

"Probably the hardest thing for people to do is to step back, slow down, and really look at themselves and recognize what they need to do to enjoy life more fully."

I think my philosophy is quite simple. I have learned to simplify my life and enjoy the things that mean the most to me. Of course, for me that means family and friends. The love of a family is priceless; they are your main support group. If you are happy in your personal life, I think everything else follows. Unfortunately, I know not everyone has this kind of support system and, consequently, I appreciate those around me that much more.

I truly try to get the most out of each day and live it to its fullest, almost as if it might be my last day. Life really is too short to "sweat the small stuff" or perhaps waste time over trivial things. I suppose everyone has different ideas about what those things might be.

Enjoy the simple things in life. Take a walk, enjoy nature; the excrcise will benefit you mentally and physically. Play with your children and really listen to them when they talk and you will always have a good relationship with them. Read a book, learn a hobby, volunteer; you'll feel better about yourself and maybe even make some new friends. Watch the sunset, the rain or the snow fall. Use your senses and be aware of everything around you. Give a smile away; you might get 10 back. Do something nice for someone and you will get so much more back.

You really need to be happy with yourself first. No person or thing can bring you happiness. You have to be able to define your own happiness and go from there. I think peace of mind will follow. Material things don't help much. People are always striving for more, sometimes living beyond their means. "The secret of contentment is knowing how to enjoy what you have," and is the one rule I live by.

Life is so fast-paced that we almost don't know how to slow down anymore and appreciate those small things in life. It's that appreciation we need to pass down to our children, along with good manners, morals and ethical values. I think some of these things are getting lost along the way, unfortunately. Probably the hardest thing for people to do is to step back, slow down, and really look at themselves and recognize what they need to do to enjoy life more fully.

Of course, the older we get, the wiser we all get. Life experiences we have change us and, hopefully, we learn from them. Losing a baby to premature birth was an episode in my life that changed things for my family. It probably brought us closer together, though I've been told it can actually break up a family. It was a very painful time in our lives and one that I will never forget, but I feel somehow richer for it. Shortly after that, our family watched helplessly as cancer ravaged a 5-year-old nephew and finally took him a year and a half later. Losing a child is one of the hardest things a parent can go through. However, these experiences somehow make us stronger.

I think religion needs to be addressed in the whole scheme of things. I'm not sure what to say but I think it's very important and has made us stronger as a family. More people should be open to it and practice it sincerely in some form.

One more thing I'd like to say. Dr. Waldinger, you talked about Dr. Ulrich and I could tell you had so much respect for him and how much you really miss him. Part of you died when he passed away. You must know that part of him still lives in you and those of us who come in contact with you every day are benefiting from that and are fortunate for it. You're a better doctor and, as a patient, I know it makes me very happy!

Commentary:

I have often noticed in my patients that the happiest ones are those who follow Mrs. Button's statement, "The secret of contentment is knowing how to enjoy what you have."

Mrs. Button also writes, "I think my philosophy is quite simple." To me it is rich with wisdom.

"There is more to life than increasing its speed."

– Mohandas Karamchand (Mahatma) Gandhi

Mrs. Carol Brinton

"Those everyday routine contacts and practices that I observed shaped my life. I'm continuing to learn and appreciate the many facets of the people who enter my life."

As the years pass, I realize that it was not always those special occasions that made an impression on my life, but the fleeting moments when I could really connect with another person, listening, sharing and caring. Those everyday routine contacts and practices that I observed shaped my life. I'm continuing to learn and appreciate the many facets of the people who enter my life.

My parents laid a good foundation for me to build upon: their example of a strong practicing religious belief, working hard to achieve their goals and not giving up, extending themselves to family and friends, and sacrificing to give my brother and me a better life than they experienced living through the Depression.

After those years of childhood scraps, I realize that my younger brother is a very loving and caring person. Seeing him achieve his educational and career goals and admiring him for having a successful marriage of 29 years have been a blessing. His and his wife's greatest accomplishment was raising two sons who are now young men who emulate good values. This was their gift to the world.

Among my friends, one woman stands out. She is so different from me in many ways and yet there is such a close bond. Her determination, thirst for learning, mind open to new ideas, a never-say-die attitude have made a big impression on my life. Seeing her overcome many hardships (spouse's addiction to alcohol, attempted suicide and subsequent divorce) has been an inspiration for me. Although she is now living in another state and we don't have the opportunity to talk as we did in the past, when we do, it's like we have never been apart.

Last, but most certainly not least, is my husband and best friend. What first attracted me to him was his calm, pleasant nature and then as we got to know one another better, his caring, love and respect. But one outstanding attribute that I must mention is his compassion for those less fortunate. He has demonstrated his concern by always putting himself in their

Carol and Bob Brinton, wedding day, 1993

place and speaking kindly of them and by giving generously to individuals and charitable organizations without ever wanting to be recognized. I am very fortunate to have these people around me. They have contributed to the philosophy I have formed.

Commentary:

One afternoon approximately five years ago, I talked with Mrs. Brinton in my office. The practice was expanding and I spoke with her regarding the need for more office space and a potential move. She took the time to listen to all of my concerns. I told her that the office held great meaning for me because of Dr. Ulrich and his legacy. She said that as long as she could drive to see me, it didn't matter where I was located. I thought for a moment and realized that the size of my office and location were clearly secondary to my ability to help my patients. The wisdom and memories of Dr. Ulrich were more important than additional space. To this day, I have stayed in the office where I first met Dr. Ulrich. My staff, patients and I always manage. Mrs. Brinton helped me that day as other people have helped her.

Mrs. Ruth Tindall

"Probably the most important lesson I learned from my mother was to accept whatever happens to me in life and make the most of it unless I can change it."

My first meaningful memories of life are during the Great Depression of the 1930s. My father died when I was 3 years old, leaving our mother with four daughters. I was the youngest. Dad had been a go-getter with a farm and a hired man, but mother was a happy-go-lucky, loving and disorganized woman. We were doomed to be poor, no matter what! In that respect, we were lucky to live during the Depression when so many others were needy, too. Probably the most important lesson I learned from my mother was to accept whatever happens to me in life and make the most of it unless I can change it.

One of my basic concerns is to please other people. When Harry and I planned to be married, we went searching for our home. After some looking, the realtor showed us one that was 50 percent above what we were willing to pay. Jokingly I said, "Oh, this is the house I want." Harry replied, "Yes, it would be just right for us." I thought, "This is the house Harry wants, too." That is how we happened to purchase our first home. It was 10 years before I learned that Harry didn't want the house either, but he thought I wanted it.

Moreover, I believe that people should be allowed to follow their own consciences, unless they interfere with others.

Commentary:

The power of love and caring for another is expressed in this wonderful story by Mrs. Ruth Tindall. It is always special in a marriage when each partner simultaneously puts the other person's wishes above his own. This occurred in Mr. and Mrs. Tindall's life and was the basis for a famous O. Henry story, "The Gift of the Magi." Our marriages and lives would be more enjoyable and more fulfilling if we learned the lessons from these stories.

Ruth and Harry Tindall, wedding portrait, 1961

Mr. & Mrs. Cornel Peleo

"Fifty years and two lovely daughters later, no sad songs for us."

Sweet Bird of Youth. The Golden Years are fleeing and memories never do.

As my husband and I reach our later years, we fondly recall the people and events that enriched our lives in the bar and restaurant business and the endless stories and Damon Runyon characters that made up our lives. We recall with amusement and sadness of all of our departed friends who played a role in our lives.

My sister marvels at how my husband can spin countless stories of "Cabbages and Kings." Our parents, born in the "old country," also added to the folklore by telling of their adventures there. Needless to say, there were a few ghosts thrown in. There are endless marathons of old movie viewing along with listening to big band albums to reminisce; and as long as we can bring a little joy to the people we come in contact with, life is good!

Fifty years and two lovely daughters later, no sad songs for us.

Commentary:

Mr. and Mrs. Peleo truly celebrate life. They know how to live in the moment. This concept is further elucidated by Robert J. Hastings in "The Station." He writes:

". . .Sooner or later we must realize there is no station, no one place to arrive at once and for all. The true joy of life is the trip. The station is only a dream. It constantly outdistances us.

"'Relish the moment' is a good motto, especially when coupled with Psalm 118:24: 'This is the day which the Lord hath made; we will rejoice and be glad in it.' It isn't the burdens of today that drive men mad. It is the regrets over yesterday and the fear of tomorrow. Regret and fear are twin thieves who rob us of today.

"So, stop pacing the aisles and counting the miles. Instead, climb more mountains, eat more ice cream, go barefoot more often, swim more rivers, watch more sunsets, laugh more, cry less. Life must be lived as we go along. The station will come soon enough."

❖

Cornel and Florence Peleo in front of her father's barber shop, Mike's Barber Shop, 245 Joseph Campau, Detroit, 1948

Love

The power and majesty of love are celebrated in the
next three philosophy of life statements.

Love is eternal–the aspect may
change, but not the essence.

– Vincent Van Gogh

Mr. & Mrs. Phil Hespen

"A Love Story—67 Years"

The "affair" started in the fourth and fifth grades. She lived two houses from him; then she moved away. But she stayed in the same school.

In junior high she should have gone to another school; instead, she walked to "our" school. Then in high school, he and she were together again for two years, attending all school social functions together. He graduated first. They were not separated because junior college classes were held in the high school.

After she graduated from high school, he went to business college and needed a job during World War II. She arranged an interview, which ended with him accepting a job. In 1944 God joined them in Holy Matrimony.

Today, this wonderful Love Story is alive and flourishing with "him" and "her" and their beautiful family of daughter and son, their spouses and three loving grandchildren.

Thank you, God, for a wonderful life! Him and Her.

Our Dear Jean

Dear Jean,

We want to share a few thoughts with you on this special weekend.

Just to let you know whatever you do or wherever you are, you will always be in our thoughts and prayers as we likewise hope to be in yours.

You have always been my buddy and my ego booster when I need it! It's just like when you make a cake or a special dish. It's the little extra something one adds which gives it the zing. That's how I like to think you have been to our lives–that extra zing which has made it special.

I hope by now since you are almost 18 that you like yourself well enough and have enough confidence in yourself to be your own person and not be swayed by what others might say or do. Think enough of yourself not to allow their methods of persuasion to impair your logical thinking and good common sense.

Love God always and include Him and His Blessed Mother in all you do, whether it be play or work, and don't forget the Golden Rule, "Do unto others as you want them to do unto you."

Love Always,
Mother and Dad

A Tribute of Love to Mom and Dad

Watching the stars from my perch
upon the bank
I feel a cold shiver invade my body.
I start to tremble
with an unreasonable fear,
a fear of what lies ahead,
the future.

I'm ending one part of my existence,
and beginning a new, more important part,
a life of my own.
But then,
I think of all you have done for me,
all you have given me;
a good set of values,
a very happy home life,
and much, much more.

You've always stood by me
and given me your love and support
when I was in need.
I feel a tide of emotions
sweep over me,
like the tide rushing
upon the beach below me.
I feel tears
gathering deep within me
as I realize, I've never fully expressed
my thanks for all you've done.

I could never think of any words
to fully convey my gratitude.

I hope with this poem,
my thoughts, feelings, and love
for you are expressed.

Love,
Jean

117

Mr. Leo Bonamy

"The way is love. Love one another. Love all you will meet today. Have no unkind words for anyone. Speak no words that you wish you never said."

Sitting on the front porch of my son Chris' house in Lexington, Michigan, with my oldest granddaughter, Wendy, we were reviewing the problems encountered by a young woman 21 years old. We talked about her life and the need to understand what may be termed a philosophy for life. Wendy, a third-year college student with a part-time job, showed concern about how to address her new experiences. She felt people were not fair. Fellow workers were only doing part of a day's work and were sitting there doing nothing when she was loaded with work. The supervisors did not seem to know what was going on or did not seem to care if it was unfair. Schoolwork took so much time. Money did not cover all of her expenses. Life was "a bummer" in her opinion. Here she sat with her grandfather. He had a nice home in Michigan where he spent his summer and a place in Florida where he spent the winter months. How could she ever plan her life to get there? It all seemed so difficult to think what could be in the future for her.

Here I sat, her 74-year-old grandfather. I had been married to a good wife who presented me with six wonderful children. She took care of the family as they grew. She kept a clean house, dressed the children well and saw that everyone was fed. As these children grew, they married and added 12 grandchildren to this world. Now it was the grandchildren's turn to make their marks on this world. Were they ready? So many problems. It was just not fair.

Years before I had had to bury my thoughts of completing my education in mechanical engineering to join my friends in World War II. I served in the U.S. Air Force with the Airborne Infantry. Called a glider specialist, I was a soldier who was armed, equipped and trained to fight on foot as well as to assemble the gliders to bring the other infantry and the equipment to the desired place at the right time. We saw service in England, France, Italy and Germany and were all expendable in the European Theatre of Operations.

Being blessed with reasonably good health, wealth and friends along the way, I have found life to be an ever-changing adventure. Loving parents worked long hours to provide me, their only child, with a modest home, simple schooling, religious ideals and a world of influences open to see. I was afforded the opportunity to evaluate each day in its turn. My philosophy of life has grown through the years not as a result of a single person or event, but from a multitude of occurrences that came along when needed to form building blocks for a future that never ends.

After I returned from the war, the first position I had was with an insurance company, and I continued my mechanical engineering schooling. My ability to read financial statements and to assess whether a contract would perform to written specifications led to my being appointed as a bond underwriter with the Fidelity and Casualty Company of New York in their Detroit office. I held this position for five years.

My interest in mechanical engineering continued to grow, and I had the opportunity to join the Hudson Motor Car Company. This move placed me not in the position of design and tooling production, but in the personnel department dealing with the review of labor problems and the assessment of work records. I assessed the records both of professionals already with the company and of those to be recruited for the company until it closed its Michigan facilities. Labor-management problems became my focal point as my career experience continued. An old classmate offered me the position of personnel manager of Mechanical Engineering Company, a steel fabricator, to work to settle differences between the unions and the company. Having completed this task, I had gained new experience with national and international applications. People problems now became the moving force in my everyday work interest.

I was next employed as Director of Personnel and worked on resolving human resources issues for the People's Community Hospital Authority. This was a system of five community hospitals bound together in 26 cities and townships in the southeastern section of Michigan. I held this position until retirement after 18 years of service to people.

A philosophy of life is never-ending. It deals with where I am today, at this time and with what that means to my world. For a youth, the plan is, or should be, to look for that schooling that will provide the tools to earn the living to have what will be wanted in the future. I feel that as an adult it is important for me

Mr. Leo Bonamy and granddaughter, Wendy, 1998

to provide for the family to the best of my ability and not to expect others to provide for them. I do not want to sit in a rocking chair and let the days roll by as a retired citizen.

What is there to do for those who will follow after me? Can the way be made better? Is it money? I think not. For in money we provide a means to material things here today, used, and tomorrow broken, trashed and gone. Is it knowledge? Of what kind? Learning how to do books or using my hands to make something? Or is it something else?

I believe it to be something else. It is to give of ourselves. What can I share with others? Time to listen. Time to be there. Suggest, help and plan. Do not direct, but share with me. Yesterday is gone. I cannot change one bit of it. What was done is done, and I cannot make it any different. It is only today and what I do today that will make any difference. Tomorrow is but the whiff of smoke that will change from what I thought it would be to something I could not see, feel or touch today.

So it is only today I have to work with. Can I make it better? That answer must be yes. The way is love. Love one another. Love all you will meet today. Have no unkind words for anyone. Speak no words that you wish you never said. I will do what work I have to do today with happiness and to the best of my ability. Once done, it may not be able to be changed. I will always speak with kind words and love others.

Commentary:

These heart-warming sentiments of Mr. Leo Bonamy lead me toward:

The Greatest of These is Love

Be ambitious for the higher gifts.
And I am going to show you a way
that is better than any of them.

If I have all the eloquence of men or of
angels, but speak without love, I am simply
a gong booming or a cymbal clashing.
If I have the gift of prophecy, understanding
all the mysteries there are, and knowing everything
and if I have faith in all its fullness, to move
mountains, but without love, then I am nothing at all.

If I give away all that I possess, piece by piece,
and if I even let them take my body to burn it, but
am without love, it will do me no good whatever.

Love is always patient and kind; it is never
jealous; love is never boastful or conceited; it is
never rude or selfish; it does not take offense,
and it's not resentful.

Love takes no pleasure in other people's sins
but delights in the truth; it is always ready to excuse,
to trust, to hope, and to endure whatever comes.

Love does not come to an end.

This is the word of the Lord.

                      – St. Paul

—— ❖ ——

C. F.

"This is why I love life."

My philosophy of life can be summed up with the following verse:

When I was young and life was still a little strange to me,
I started to formulate my own philosophy.

And yet, it was not all my own,
For much of it was part of all the songs and happy dreams
That fill the human heart.

I wanted to be kind and good and faithful to each vow
And do as much for others as the hours would allow.

I wanted to serve my God and country and be worthy of my wife
And to educate our children to the finer things in life.

And, if today, I have some cause for happiness and pride,
It is because of God's good grace and I know that I have tried.

There are many sorrows in this life.
There are many more pleasures. This is why I love life.

Commentary:

For as long as I can remember, a very special patient has called me during the first week of December for my list of holiday poinsettia recipients. He personally selects and delivers each of these plants to homes and offices throughout Dearborn and outlying communities.

When I read his inspiring poem, I understood why he calls me each December. As his poem states, he wants to "do as much for others as they would allow." I have always been very grateful to him for his kindness, generosity and caring.

"It is well to think well; it is divine to act well."

– Horace Mann

Father John Canavan

*"My legacy is simple. I want to be remembered as a very
human person who held on to his dreams and goals.
Also, a person who has reached out to touch the lives
of others with gentle love."*

I was born in late December of 1926. My parents experienced
the joys and the trials of raising me and my sister along with
my two brothers. The love they had for each other and their role
as parents were tested during the years of the Great Depression.

The marriage of my parents took place in St. Peter and Paul's
Church, county Asmagh, Northern Ireland. Dad was a
Protestant, and mother a Catholic. This marriage presented no
bitterness between them. Dad became a Catholic and faithful in
his religious responsibilities. He set a good example to his children. Often he entertained us by singing hymns from his early
childhood. Later, on my journey as a parish priest, the ecumeni-
cal attitude that I was taught motivated me to help bring some
harmony between Catholics and Christians of other persuasions.

My sister, Marie, after graduating from junior high school,
took a trip to Ireland. Both mother and daughter were thrilled
with the visit. The anticipation of their arrival helped to dimin-
ish the fears of the seven-day boat trip. They also experienced
the joy with relatives and friends. However, a sudden, unexpected illness brought death to my sister. The cause of death was
diabetes. Mother's trip back to the States was filled with deep
sorrow and grief. I was too young at age 10 to feel empathy

toward my mother. This tragedy left me without a sister—a sister who would have been extremely helpful to me in my priesthood. A beautiful framed picture of my sister hangs on the wall of my cottage/retirement home, which is an ever-present reminder of a special person in my family.

My formal education came from the public schools in east Dearborn. A helping hand was extended to me with the invitation to attend Henry Ford Trade School. These were delightful days for me as I enjoyed working and learning the skills of the automotive profession. Apart from the education, I gained a deep appreciation of the teachers. They treated me and the other students as their sons. In my reflection later in life, I realized that it was my duty to give back a portion of myself as I had been blessed by others.

After graduation in January 1945, I was drafted into the service. I volunteered for the paratroopers after basic training. Later, I was assigned as a chaplain's assistant. In admiration of the good done by the chaplain, I was motivated to pursue a call to life in the priesthood. My mother was delighted to hear of my decision to go to the seminary. College life was a big challenge for me. But with perseverance, prayers and faithful work, I was able to be ordained a priest of the Diocese of Detroit in June 1955. As a parish priest over these past 44 years, I have touched the lives of countless thousands of people. Apart from the diversity in race, color, culture and creed, we all share so much in common. We are all pilgrim people. They have taught me a great deal of the realities of life—the joys, the hopes, the needs, the challenges and especially, the pain of our struggles.

My assignment in the Diocese began at St. John's Church in Monroe. After one year at the parish, I was sent to St. Joseph's Parish in Erie to work among the Hispanic migrants. The following parishes that I served after a period of sickness due to migraine headaches were: St. Lawrence in Utica, St. Syril in Taylor, St. Basil in Eastpointe, and then pastor of St. Constance Church in Taylor. As pastor of the parish for 27 years, I fulfilled my duties to the best of my abilities. The guidelines of Vatican II, which opened the doors and windows of the Church, gave me the encouragement to help implement the teachings of Catholicism. This effort helped bring about a further sign of our Lord's presence to our community.

My housekeeper, Patricia, was a great blessing to me and to the people of the parish. She never complained about her paralysis. She was a person of living faith, a saintly person, and a wonderful friend. She suffered a major stroke at the age of 83. As her caregiver, I experienced the challenge

Father John Canavan, 1997

of doing whatever I was able to do to ease her pain and suffering. One of the lessons I learned from the many visits to her nursing home is that caring for your loved one has a price. The price was an expression of my love and deep appreciation for her.

In my journey as a parish priest, I sensed the formation and development of my personal value system. I believe that people want to be loved, respected and accepted. I believe that people have been blessed with many gifts and talents. People also have many needs and wants. Perhaps my words and signs of affirmation have helped uplift those I touched. I am also aware of my needs, especially friendship. I have learned to be a giving person with "unconditional love," and to "give back" by showing my appreciation for what people have done for me is something always on my mind.

My legacy is simple. I want to be remembered as a very human person who held on to his dreams and goals and also, as a person who has reached out to touch the lives of others with gentle love. As the Israelites journeyed some 40 years in the desert seeking and longing for God's love, so too I journey. I journey with a human heart to be nourished by others. I also journey, mindful of my stumbling disappointments, pains and challenges, but with a song in my heart. I don't know where my journey will take me, but it is my journey.

Commentary:

To know Father Canavan and to call him "friend" is to be among the fortunate. Father Canavan has been a source of comfort for me. His wisdom is a permanent source of comfort for all.

> ". . .the only true gift is a
> portion of thyself."

> – Ralph Waldo Emerson

Mr. Arthur Shaw

"We finished the hole and as we walked off the green, I broke the silence with, 'Don, you had a problem.' "

I learned my philosophy of life from a very dear friend named Don Merryman. This man influenced my life in so many ways and the effect that he had on me was truly profound. His attitude toward life was wonderful. He was interested in people and his philosophy made me change the way I experienced life and how I was able to cope with all the challenges that I had to face.

Playing golf with my friend Don Merryman was always an enjoyable experience. Don carried a 12 handicap at three country clubs—Washtenaw, Dearborn and Whispering Pines, North Carolina. Playing golf with Don on a sunny day at Washtenaw was an event that I wish to share with you. On the 15th hole, par 4, Don had a fine drive through the woods straight down the center of the fairway. However, his second shot was short of the green and the ball went into the water fronting the green. Don quietly opened a sleeve of new Titleist balls and promptly hit the next three into the water. He then followed with the second and third sleeves of three. He also proceeded to take the fourth sleeve out of his bag without a word and went on to hit three beautiful shots near the hole. We finished the hole and as we walked off the green, I broke the silence with, "Don, you had a problem." He answered, "Yes, but I solved my problem."

Don was a gentleman in every way. In our 30 years of friendship, he never used off-color words and never spoke of anyone except in a positive way. He also never told a joke that could not be heard by everyone. I wonder what he would think about our TV programs, our newspapers and our world leaders and their actions today. Don's expression of anger was "Dad bum it!"

He and his family visited all of our states. He wanted his children to know and see all of the country he loved. My wife, Maxine, and I built a home in Whispering Pines, North Carolina, next to Hazel and Don's with the desire to enjoy their friendship for many years. The loss of Don changed everything. We sold our home of 10 years, never to have lived in it.

A friend of his of about four years called me after we lost Don and said, "Art, I must tell you how I felt about your friend." He said, "If a man can love a man, I loved Don." I loved this special man also. Don was close to his church and his contact with all people was one of caring. His years of work and service as a Rotarian, I believe, tell much of this man.

Maxine and Arthur Shaw, 1975

Commentary:

Patients have shared many golf stories with me over the years. It's enjoyable to watch their excitement when they say they have hit a hole in one. Mr. Shaw's golf story is the best I have heard. Mr. Merryman's approach to a difficult situation was impressive. He handled this shot with grace and composure. Then, in a calm and elegant manner, he practiced to solve his problem. Mr. Shaw discussed that golfers can get very upset over a bad shot. Mr. Merryman's approach to a difficulty had a profound effect on Mr. Shaw. Mr. Shaw internalized the lesson learned from Mr. Merryman's action and, consequently, he was better able to approach difficulties in his own life.

Mrs. Arthur Shaw (left), golfing with the Merrymans, 1970

Mrs. Irene Panter

"It never entered my mind that one day I might have to give up my rose-colored glasses and deal with the real world."

I wore rose-colored glasses as a young girl. Life was wonderful during my youth. It never entered my mind that one day I might have to give up my rose-colored glasses and deal with the real world. Life was not always easy. What a shock! I was not prepared to cope with the difficult challenges that came with marriage, children, serious illness and death. Those problems were often fought with tears of frustration.

Eventually, I learned that time, patience and, most of all, faith were the solution to my dilemmas. Those three key words have seen me through some very stressful years and I am grateful to have survived and feel that I am a stronger person today as a result.

My mother taught me that life is good in spite of the trauma along the way. She truly loved life and squeezed every ounce of happiness she could from it. Her wonderful spirit will always be with me as I make my way through my Golden Years.

Commentary:

The wisdom that we have learned from our life experiences can help another. This is clearly demonstrated when Mrs. Irene

Panter writes, "Eventually, I learned that time, patience and, most of all, faith were the solution to my dilemmas." Mrs. Panter's mother also influenced her philosophy of life: "She truly loved life and squeezed every ounce of happiness she could from it." The process of helping another in a time of uncertainty, grief or mourning can bring clarity and resolution to personal dilemmas. Solutions to personal problems can come from unexpected places.

Harold S. Kushner provides an example of this concept in his book, *When Bad Things Happen to Good People*, when he writes,

"There is an old Chinese tale about the woman whose only son died. In her grief, she went to the holy man and said, 'What prayers, what magical incantations do you have to bring my son back to life?' Instead of sending her away or reasoning with her, he said to her, 'Fetch me a mustard seed from a home that has never known sorrow. We will use it to drive the sorrow out of your life.' The woman set off at once in search of that magical mustard seed. She came first to a splendid mansion, knocked at the door, and said, 'I am looking for a home that has never known sorrow. Is this such a place? It is very important to me.' They told her, 'You've certainly come to the wrong place,' and began to describe all the tragic things that had recently befallen them. The woman said to herself, 'Who is better able to help these poor unfortunate people than I, who have had misfortune of my own?' She stayed to comfort them, then went on in her search for a home that had never known sorrow. But wherever she turned, in hovels and in palaces, she found one tale after another of sadness and misfortune. Ultimately, she became so involved in ministering to other people's grief that she forgot about her quest for the magical mustard seed, never realizing that it had in fact driven the sorrow out of her life."

❖

Anonymous Patient

"Pass it on. . ."

After much thought, I have decided there are several instances that helped form my philosophy of life. I am a Depression baby and was born in 1933. We lived in a suburb of Detroit and, as for most people during the Depression, money was short. Thank goodness, my dad was fortunate. He had a job that was necessary. This position was shared with two other people. The company they worked for allowed them each to work one day a week. Instead of two having no income, each had one day's pay. This helped with the necessities, but there was nothing left over for extras. I had an aunt who had no children, but had a steady job and was very generous. She provided us with many things whenever she could. The Depression ended, we grew up and help from our aunt was no longer necessary. However, she was always around and always willing to help.

When my husband and I were married, he had just completed college, but I had not yet finished. He was from another state and I had not yet met his family. Money was very scarce. My aunt, however, was aware that we would like to make the trip to see his family. We were not sure that we could afford to travel, even by car. My generous aunt provided the means for the trip as a wedding present. My husband and I were very grateful, but

134

did not know how we could ever repay her for her help throughout our life. She looked surprised and said, "Well, you were
never expected to repay me. You are, however, expected to 'pass
it on' if it is needed and if you are able."

My husband and I took this advice seriously. Throughout our
life together, we have had several relatives who needed assistance and whenever we were able, we did "pass it on." I realized
one day to my delight that we had indeed "passed it on." Not
only had we helped when possible, but also we must have passed
the philosophy on to the next generation. Shortly after our
daughter had married, there was a family gathering for our son-
in-law's family. Apparently one of his younger relatives needed
some help, and he and our daughter were providing some assistance. His father was cautioning him that they probably would
not be repaid. Our son-in-law answered, "Oh, we do not expect
to be repaid. My wife's family has a tradition that if one can
afford to help, one does and, if repayment is not possible, then
those helped should pass it on when they can."

My aunt died several years ago. We are very grateful that her
philosophy has lived on and helped many others. Hopefully, the
next generation will continue the philosophy started by my aunt
years ago. It has been a lesson well learned.

Commentary:

This philosophy reminds me of the knowledge, love and wisdom that Dr. Ulrich "passed on" to me.

In *Lines Composed a Few Miles Above Tintern Abbey*, William
Wordsworth writes of the kindness of unassuming, generous
everyday people.

> "The best portion of a good man's life,
> His little, nameless, unremembered acts
> Of kindness and of love."

❖

Grandma's Wisdom

The philosophy of life statements of Mrs. Geraldine Robbins and Mrs. Margaret Vanderwill are based on their grandmothers. There can be such great wisdom learned from our grandparents. I am so grateful that Mrs. Robbins and Mrs. Vanderwill shared their "Grandma's Wisdom."

May the source of strength who blessed the
ones before us, help us find the courage to make
our lives a blessing, and let us say; Amen.

— Debbie Friedman

❖

Mrs. Geraldine Robbins

*"To this day, I have tears in my eyes when I remember
these and other sayings of this gracious and kind woman
who raised a child when she was 50 years old."*

I was born an only child of a woman in the process of divorcing
my father. I have never met my father. When I was born, my
maternal immigrant Swedish grandma cried, "What will
become of this baby?" In those early days, people with mental
weaknesses, called "nerves," had no medicines to help them
function successfully in society. It was 1931, and my mother
wanted no part in caring for me. Her only sibling, a sister 13
months younger, replied, "Don't cry; something good will come
of this child. We will all take care of her." So began my journey
in life with four caretakers: my maternal grandpa and grandma
and my dear aunt and uncle.

I loved all four of my caretakers, and they were all so very
good and kind to me. My aunt and uncle took me traveling with
them and their only child, my cousin, a girl two and one-half
years younger than I. We grew up as close as sisters could have
been. I spent summers with them as much as with my grandparents. I never missed the "normal" family I didn't have. It wasn't
until I had a husband, two sons, and a dog of my own that I lived
in a family like those I had seen as a child.

My mother was a shadow in the background. Sometimes she
was able to be in society and use her teaching degree. Other

times, she was back living with my grandparents and me. However, all of my values and philosophies about life were pronouncements from my dear grandma.

"Don't say anything if you don't have anything good to say." "The years go faster when you get older." "You were born so that your husband, such an ambitious and helpful person with so many talents, could help us in our old age." He loved my grandparents and helped grandpa maintain many properties which he had built and rented. My husband ate my grandma's voluminous cooking with glee.

"We old people have to die off to make room for more babies to be born and have a place on this earth. That is God's plan." "Oh, I am so happy to see children eat. In the old country, we had so little to eat." (This statement might include a pinch on the cheeks of my young sons!) "Always be kind and gentle to people and animals. They all have feelings." "We don't know why your mother is the way she is. But be very quiet, and be nice to her. She can't help the way she is."

As I grew older, I was more aware of mental problems in people than any friends of mine were. I tried to understand and be kind and helpful. This ability has helped me in my own trying personal circumstances.

I was 54 when my first husband died in a sudden accident. He had been a loving husband and father to the three of us. We were all left with empty spaces in our lives, from which my two sons have never recovered. However, they are happy that I met a fine man and remarried after two and one-half years of widowhood. He is an engineer just as their dad was, and my younger son is. They all worked in the iron and steel industry. I was also formally educated in engineering, rare for the '50s, but dedicated my life to teaching middle school children math and science.

Grandma would say, "God has plans for our lives. We may not know what they are, but we will know when we look back." I think about her wise words often as I relive my husband's death and my meeting and marrying for a second time.

"Always be clean, dress nice, and do the best you can. We came to this country with two empty hands, and we worked

Mrs. Geraldine Robbins (right) and her cousin, 1938

from dawn to dusk to get what we have." From their examples, I learned a strong work ethic, which I applied to my education to get the best grades possible. Then I worked with diligence around my home and still enjoy every minute of that. I always thought I earned my paycheck when I was teaching school, because I used the God-given talents of creativity and ambition to create stimulating educational activities for my students.

"I need to bring food to my neighbors. They are hungry, and we are not. Help me bring this over." I have continued cooking "too much" every since those days I helped grandma. She taught me to knit and crochet, to bake and cook, to entertain and clean up! She taught me to help paint rooms, to sweep up messes grandpa made as he built, and to get dirty working. No task was too much work or beneath her. Life was adventurous as you participated in the event; picking wild blueberries was a time of laughter and shared time on our knees.

To this day, I have tears in my eyes when I remember these and other sayings of this gracious and kind woman who raised a child when she was 50 years old. The Lord took her gently when she was 80 years old, with a one-week coma after a stroke. We buried her with a funeral that included a hymn so loved by the Swedes, "How Great Thou Art."

❖

Mrs. Margaret Vanderwill

"Grandma was a gem—not only for her courage in dealing with difficulties and hardships, but for her love of life and all people."

My philosophy of life was greatly influenced by my maternal grandmother. She was a most loving and compassionate person. She had a very meaningful life filled with incredible challenges, grief and joy.

My grandmother inspired me for my entire life. When I was approximately eight years old, she began to introduce me to the beautiful things in the world. Her lovely manners, grace and ability to celebrate the happy experiences in life were remarkable.

I recall a very special occasion when we went to a tea at the Henry Ford Mansion. My memories are so vivid that I can still see Mrs. Ford serving tea from a lovely teapot. The petite tea sandwiches and exquisite little tea cookies were delicious. The massive table was covered with an elegant lace cloth. I was so impressed. As I reflect back, I feel that this charming event inspired my love for beautiful things and happy times.

However, my remarkable grandmother had another side to her dynamic personality. She was so kind to the poor and the sick. Her example taught me that I could be a complete person and experience the full spectrum of life's offerings. Grandma inspired me to enjoy it all and live a life filled with meaning and purpose.

During the Depression, grandma would work all day in her own home helping individuals find work, getting clothes for their children, and assisting them in keeping their bills paid. In fact, she became one of the first registered social workers in western Wayne County.

After a hard day's work and no compensation, grandma would pick me up and drive to the St. Joseph's Retreat at Michigan Avenue and Outer Drive. She would get pans of hot soup and homemade bread from the Sisters of Charity and deliver food to the poor residing in the outskirts of Dearborn. This act of kindness would occur after 7:30 p.m. when the patients at the Retreat were all fed and leftovers were available.

Grandma was a gem—not only for her courage in dealing with difficulties and hardships, but for her love of life and all people. Color or religion did not matter to this exceptional woman. She felt that each individual was a valuable human being.

Her mission and vision certainly influenced my life. I became a registered nurse and strived to emulate her. Her profound ability to balance human service along with enjoying the beauty of everyday life has always inspired me. Grandma taught me to be the best I could be, care deeply for all people and their enduring issues, and that inner strength is a gift of faith.

❖

Mrs. Margaret Vanderwill's grandmother,
Mary K. Moody Buckenberger, 1895

Family

The next philosophy of life statements center on the importance of family in our lives. It is remarkable that my patients were able to give so much to their family members and friends despite the hardships and problems they encountered. They all learned something different that they returned to humanity.

My family has been the greatest joy in my life. They have been a continual source of support and I have learned much from them. Dr. and Mrs. Ulrich and my patients have been my extended family.

I close this section with two birthday letters and poems written for my children.

Mrs. Iva Billig

"My father worked the land and this allowed him to have spiritual connections with God and a deep respect for all God's creations. My mother followed the same path."

I was born May 12, 1920, in the small town of West Branch, Michigan. My family consisted of five sisters and one brother. My parents were farmers and did a lot of hard work for little income. The most important factor in our lives was that my parents gave us all a lot of love. We were able to become emotionally secure and feel a sense of well-being. Early on in life we accepted that material things would be scarce and we had to learn to make do and share with others.

Religion played an important role in our lives. My father worked the land and this allowed him to have spiritual connections with God and a deep respect for all God's creations. My mother followed the same path. Therefore, by the example set for us by such wonderful and devoted parents, I would like to think we grew up to be well-balanced individuals with respect for God and our fellowman.

When it came time for high school, it was difficult for us to get to the school without transportation being available. As a result, my parents located a good family where we could stay during the week and work for our room and board. We were able to go home only on weekends. After graduating from high school, I decided to go into nursing. Looking back, I realized this wasn't so unusual. It was probably due to the example set for me by my parents. Their kindness and willingness to help all people made me realize I also wanted to help others. There is no better way to accomplish this than by being a nurse.

I'd like to relate this incident to you about how my parents were able to help someone. One day a young man approximately 15 or 16 years of age stopped at my parents' home and asked if he could stay the night. Of course, my parents said, "Yes." He spent the evening enjoying a good home-cooked meal and a discussion of what happened to each of us that day. The next morning he left. Thirty-five years later when my parents were celebrating their Golden Wedding anniversary, they received a card in the mail. In it the writer said, "You may not remember me but I spent one night in your home and that night changed the whole course of my life. I was running away from home and the example your family set for me made me decide to turn around and go back. I now am happily married and have several children and am eternally grateful to you."

I met and married Robert Billig in 1952. We have four beautiful children: Judy, Barbara, Michael and Jean. Throughout my life I probably was involved in nursing on and off for 35 years. I always enjoyed doing for others and still do. My husband died in April of 1996. We were married for 43 years. I now have another big adjustment in my life–learning to live alone. However, with my faith and trust in God and my four wonderful children, I know I will manage.

Mrs. Sara Montemurri

*"It is a coincidence that both my cousin and mother
shared the same birthday–November 11."*

My mother, Grace Montemurri (nee Caruso), was born on
November 18, 1905, in Detroit. She was one of nine children born to Joseph and Angeline Caruso. On December 2,
1922, at the age of 17, she married my father, Angelo Montemurri, a marriage that lasted over 50 years. The Depression
years were a struggle but they survived the hardships, with
mother taking in boarders to help them out financially. She
cooked, cleaned, washed clothes by hand, and did the ironing.
She thought nothing of washing walls, shoveling snow and cutting the grass. She did whatever needed to be done.

In spite of her great strength and spirit and all the hardships
she endured, she was extremely nervous when she first went to
see Dr. Waldinger. However, his caring and soothing manner
soon put her at ease. In subsequent visits, she was much less
apprehensive.

She led a caring, giving life and her greatest joy was her family. Nothing was too much to do for them. When she reached the
age of 86, she was diagnosed with renal failure and given six
weeks to live. My brother and I took care of her at home for a
while, but then decided that it would be better for her to go to a
hospice facility. She surprised everyone and survived for eight

months thanks to the wonderful care she received. While there, she was a favorite with all the staff, always cheerful, giving advice and sharing her recipes. She was a wonderful Italian cook with everything homemade, including bread, pasta, etc.

On September 12, 1994, she passed away, beloved by all her family and friends. When I called my cousin in Syracuse, New York, she immediately made plans to attend the funeral. It is a coincidence that both my cousin and mother shared the same birthday–November 11. However, the next morning my cousin injured her knee and had to be taken to the hospital for surgery. Mother's funeral was the same day as her surgery. My cousin was nervous and upset that she could not be with us for the funeral. However, as my cousin was being wheeled into the operating room, a nurse came to her and held her hand. She said, "My name is Grace. Don't be afraid. We'll take good care of you." My cousin was comforted and knew that Aunt Grace was taking care of her family, looking down from Heaven.

Mrs. Sara Montemurri and great-granddaughter, Lauren, 1990

Mr. Walter Piotrowski

*"It wasn't until I was older that I understood that the love
and concern that my parents had for me caused them to
go into debt in order to pay for my medical expenses."*

My name is Walter Piotrowski. I am 71 years of age and
married to Mary, my wife of 44 years. We are the proud
parents of four children–Wally, Gregory, Kevin and Marianne–
and the grandparents of Alexandra and Matthew.

I believe that my philosophy of life and the living and col-
lected wisdoms that have resulted have been influenced by
many varied experiences. However, most of them have been
directly related to the examples set by my parents.

I have been afflicted with a dermatological condition called
psoriasis since the age of five and have also experienced several
other skin problems. My initial involvement with psoriasis was
in 1932. It wasn't long before my entire body was one large itchy
scab. As I recall, it seemed that at the time no one really understood what it was or its cause. Proper treatment and a possible
cure were not yet known. As a youngster, I'm sure I wasn't aware
that my parents couldn't afford to pay for the medicines, salves,
treatments and doctor's fees to treat my skin condition. It wasn't
until I was older that I understood that the love and concern that
my parents had for me caused them to go into debt in order to
pay for my medical expenses.

My parents' dedication to family went beyond just my concerns, but included caring for my siblings as well as other relatives. Their many years of sacrifice, dedication and endurance have definitely influenced and shaped my life and its associated wisdoms. I am who I am in part because of their examples as well as their love of life. I know that being raised in this environment has over the years given me the wisdom to be tolerant, generous and loving. The validity of this outlook on life and living has for me been proven time and again as a great foundation for establishing wonderful relationships.

The other part of who I am has to do with my wife who, over the years, has not only shared, but also often exceeded this outlook on life and its meaning. All of this makes me realize the importance of the wisdom of the lifestyle we all attempt to live by.

Mr. Walter Piotrowski (right) and his father with their "catch of the day," 1939

Mrs. Lucienne Gosselin

"Up until then, she was still knitting sweaters for needy children all over the world."

I was born in Thetford-Mines, Quebec, and moved to the United States with my husband and three children when I was 34 years old. Perhaps the one person who taught me the most and had the strongest influence on my life was the woman who raised me, Caroline Perreault. I had three older brothers and an older sister. My mother died giving birth to me so I never knew her. The woman I think of as "mother" came into my life after having suffered as many tests and setbacks as a human could be expected to endure.

Mother had been married at a young age and was widowed after 10 years. She moved to the U.S. and worked in a shoe box factory in Manchester, New Hampshire, for the next several years. One day she received a request from the sister of her deceased husband. This poor woman, pregnant with her ninth child, had just become a widow herself. Her husband died in a mining accident. Caroline didn't hesitate. She went back to Quebec immediately to help. Her sister-in-law then died and Caroline ended up caring for these children for the next two years.

My father, having been a widower for two years, asked Caroline to marry him and she agreed. Then she had two children with my father and I now had two younger sisters.

Mrs. Lucienne Gosselin and her mother, Mrs. Caroline Perreault, Quebec City, 1970

Mother was very wise. My mother was from the "spare the rod, spoil the child" school of child raising. Whenever one of us kids did something wrong, mother would wait until they went to bed before telling father about it. That way, he usually didn't hand out such a strict punishment. A good night's rest tempered his response to the transgression.

She and father were married for 16 years before he died of tuberculosis. Again, this woman found herself a widow raising seven children. She taught us many things–the most important of all being "love and caring" for others. The woman I knew as "mother" was with us until she died at the age of 95. Up until then, she was still knitting sweaters for needy children all over the world.

Mrs. Flora Gorman

*"If I do nearly as well as they did, the Lord will be well
pleased with me, too."*

I was born 65 years ago in a tiny Italian village about 90 miles
south of Rome. Although I lived there only two years, that
community, its culture and ethnicity shaped my life and greatly
influenced every aspect of the person I am today.

The little village, named Pietrafita, could not support all of its
families, few as they were. My parents, brother, two sisters and I
lived with our paternal grandparents on their farm. Grandpa's
land provided only enough food to feed our household. During a
good year a few crops might bring in just enough money to buy
fabric for our meager clothes, and perhaps enough for one pair
of shoes for the two or three lucky family members who needed
them most. (My husband says that explains what he calls my
"shoe fetish.")

It was clear to my dad, long before I was born, (I am the
youngest of the four children, 16 years younger than my brother,
and 14 and 12 years younger than my sisters, respectively) that
he could not provide the kind of life he wanted for his family in
Italy. He began then to seek his fortune in Rome, Spain,
England and the United States of America.

After many trips back to Italy, he finally convinced my
mother that America offered the best opportunity for a better

155

life for all of us. She was naturally reluctant, being 45 years old at the time, having to leave her mother, relatives, friends and the only culture and language she knew.

In October of 1935, when I was two years old, we left for America. Certainly 1935 was not a good year in any city in the United States. There were hard times, many hard years, but dad, having survived the union wars at the Ford Motor Company in Dearborn, was able to seek out a life that was ultimately better than what we had in our little Italian village.

My parents' work ethic rubbed off on all of us children. We all worked hard at whatever we did. My sisters married at the tender ages of 17 and 18, disappointing my parents by not getting a higher education, but pleasing them by working very hard at being good spouses, parents and homemakers. My brother also disappointed them by not going to college, but they were very proud of him when he became one of the vice presidents of a major auto parts company.

I achieved a Master's Degree in Elementary Education and it was a great source of pride for my parents and for me. I'm delighted that they lived to see my two sons and several of my siblings' children receive college diplomas. That was the fulfillment of the American dream they had for their family.

At mom and dad's funerals, the eulogist, said: "He, (She) fought the good fight, ran the race, and it is finished. In him, (her) I know the Lord is well pleased." I thank them every day for having the courage to pull up their roots and travel to a new country and for all the sacrifices that entailed, in order to give us an opportunity for a better life.

I thank God for the gift of having had two such loving parents and for all the blessings He has bestowed on me and my loved ones. Every day I can see something of my parents in my thoughts, actions, behaviors, and in those of my sons, Mark and Bill, and even in those of my five grandchildren. Mom and dad taught me, by example, how to walk in the ways of the Lord and I'm trying to do the same for my family. If I do nearly as well as they did, the Lord will be well pleased with me, too.

❖

Mrs. Florence Litogot

*"My grandmother and grandfather would always make
sure that even though their customers had no money, they
could still get groceries at their store."*

My maternal and paternal grandparents and my mother
were born in Europe. My maternal grandfather came to
the United States first because of the oppression in Europe and
opportunities available in the United States. He secured an
apartment and job in New York, saved his money and booked
third-class passage on the *Titanic* for my mother, who was one
year old, and my grandmother. During their long journey on the
train to the boat, my grandmother became ill and missed the
boat. They then booked passage on another ship. They were
never listed among the survivors or the deceased on the *Titanic*.
My grandfather presumed they had perished. However, when
my mother and grandmother arrived in New York unannounced, needless to say there was much celebration. My father
was the eldest of 13 children and had a twin sister who died in
infancy. The remaining 11 siblings were all boys. My mother
was the eldest of seven. I am an only child.

During my mother's and father's courtship, both families
became very close. I was born five years after my parents' marriage. I was born at home and was a breech birth. That was very
difficult for my petite mother. All of my aunts, uncles and
cousins were very close to me while I was growing up. Every

holiday, birthday and anniversary would be celebrated by both families. It was a wonderful, close family experience for me.

When I was growing up, my mother's parents owned a meat market/grocery store. From the age of 12 through high school, I worked in their store and learned a lot about human kindness and how to treat people properly. My grandmother and grandfather would always make sure that even though their customers had no money, they could still get groceries at their store. We wrote their name in an account book and whether or not they paid made no difference to my grandparents. No one ever went hungry who shopped at their store. This act of human kindness has remained with me my entire life.

I attended college, married and had three children. The first child died at birth. I worked in the medical field and found it to be very rewarding. However, it eventually became too demanding with two small children to raise, so I obtained a marketing position at Michigan Bell Telephone. I was promoted to manager and then went to AT&T and later to Lucent Technologies where I took a special early retirement.

Mrs. Florence Litogot, 1998

I am currently in charge of community service work for my company in a tri-state region. We are involved in education, donations of equipment for the handicapped, installing telecommunications systems for charitable organizations, food donations and the Special Olympics. I also do volunteer fund raising and public speaking for the American Cancer Society. I have been selected to serve on my church council and am involved in religious education for adults.

I feel that my parents and extended family have made me a very strong and independent woman. At this stage in my life, I feel that God has blessed me so much that I want to give back to the community and others less fortunate with my time, wisdom, love and caring. I believe that with a positive mental attitude, a never-give-up philosophy and the fact that age is no more than a number, one can accomplish anything.

Mr. Richard Moore

*"When his mother called and told me I am his hero,
I was floored!"*

To be considerate of family members and people you come in contact with throughout your lifetime is the basis of my philosophy. What a challenge!

As a father of five children–one son and four daughters–plus a grandfather of 20 grandchildren–10 boys and 10 girls, the oldest 16 and the youngest one year of age–I have to be aware of what I say and know that the actions I take will be an example to all of them as they grow up.

It wasn't until I went into the service that I realized how much my father's philosophy and values influenced my life. I joined the Marine Corps during the Korean War–the most disciplined and strictest branch of the service at the time. During Boot Camp, I wrote my dad and thanked him for the example he had set for me as I grew up. The training got me through Boot Camp and also my years in the Corps. I try to set the same example for my kids–in work, with people and with their own family members.

My work ethic has always been to give 100 percent to my employer, regardless of the job. In the 42 years I enjoyed with one employer and seven with another, I can honestly say I always did my very best. I have seen this same standard carried

Mr. Richard Moore, 1998

on by my own son, daughters, and my sons-in-law. Now I see my grandkids doing the same, whether it is in school, work, sports, or just household chores.

It's easy to quote the Golden Rule but to follow it is often difficult. I have tried to instill its meaning in my family by example, in regard to all people. There is no greater compliment, as far as I'm concerned, than to overhear my kids or grandkids say, "Grandpa says," or "Grandpa would have done it this way." Just recently, one of my grandsons, age nine, had to do a school project. He had to build a monument and explain its meaning to his classmates. The monument was to be of his number one hero. When his mother called and told me I am his hero, I was floored!

To make mistakes and to admit them, and to help people without seeking payment or recognition are other examples I try to set. As the years go by, it's very gratifying to know that you've made a difference in the way so many lives have been shaped. Philosophy and values go pretty much hand in hand. I think I have unconsciously given mine to at least 30 people I know of, and hopefully a lot more.

❖

Mrs. Harriet Sawyer

"I will be with you always."

After only 12 years of marriage, my minister husband died suddenly, leaving me to raise three children alone. When my mind and emotions cleared, I realized we would have to find a place to live because we were living in the church parsonage at that time. I also knew I needed surgery in the near future. The last straw broke when our eldest child fell from the monkey bars at school, fractured his upper arm and had to spend a month in traction at Children's Hospital. "Dear God," I cried. "This is more than I can handle. Too many needs! Not a clue, no direction!"

I had always been independent, even in childhood. A good friend recently reminded me that my mother died when I was only 15 and my dad and I had managed alone, leaving me pretty much on my own through high school and part of my college days.

This was different, I thought. I was devastated and desperate. I had forgotten the strength of family and friends. "First things first," one of them said. Our first break came when an acquaintance stopped by, offering to help us find a new place to live. Together we located a cozy house in Dearborn and it was just a perfect size. We moved in the week before Christmas and it became our home for 40 years.

My first born child entered the first grade and I had the surgery that same spring. The following fall, number two entered kindergarten. At about the same time, I was offered a part-time position in an area of interest to me. It turned into a full-time position and I stayed at the same job for 15 years. But, what about the baby? Before I accepted the position, a kind and caring lady literally appeared on our doorstep and became a substitute mother and housekeeper for our family. How lucky could we be? She grew so attached to us that she continued to stay with us off and on until the children finished high school and then college. She even attended one of their weddings!

During the children's early years, I occasionally talked to them about their father, reminding them of things he had said and done. This was to help them remember him and, in the beginning, to aid in their grief. "Do you think he knows what's happening to us?" the oldest asked. I replied that I was sure of an awareness because dad's love was strong–it was eternal. Then I read them the engraved message inside my wedding ring–"I will be with you always." It had been close to me for many of the past difficult years.

The children are grown now with children of their own and I am finding how great it is to be a grandparent. Recently, one of the college-aged grandsons was telling me about a girl he had met in school. He is very much in love and hopes someday to marry her. Then he asked about his granddad and me. I showed him the well-worn band on my finger. He was thrilled to be able to make out the lettering; "I will be with you always."

Suddenly I had a flash of insight. That was it. The message on the ring was not my husband's alone. They are the final words of Jesus at the end of the book of St. Matthew when He says, "For lo, I will be with you always, even until the end of the world!"

How wonderful can life be!

My acquaintance with Dr. Ulrich was limited to one or two appointments. Near the Thanksgiving holiday, I waited in a small examining room. As Dr. Ulrich was leaving a patient in the next room the door was slightly open and I heard him say, "By the way, what are you doing on Thanksgiving?" I could not hear

the patient's reply but the doctor said, "Fine, have a good day."
Then he came into my room. After treatment, he smiled and
asked, "By the way, where will you be on Thanksgiving?" I told
him I was invited to a home of a family member. "Have a
blessed day," was his reply. It was then that I realized Dr. Ulrich
was inviting each patient that day to have Thanksgiving dinner
with him and his family. I wish I had known him better.

Mrs. Harriett Sawyer, 1996

Mr. & Mrs. Robert Briggs

"They were born and raised on an island and rest to eternity on an island."

One month in 1955 I interviewed on tape my mother and dad, my grandfather (Edward Neusesser) and Jennie's folks (Christine and David Bruce) to get their life stories. I conducted the interviews to satisfy my curiosity about a way of life that was fading from their memories. The interview with Jennie's parents was particularly interesting.

At first mom was reluctant to talk about the past, preferring to "let sleeping dogs lie," so to speak. As David told stories and answered questions, she got caught up in the spirit of the interview and became quite loquacious. At the end she recovered her taciturn character and indignantly asked, "Why are we telling you all these things?"

I didn't respond but rewound the tape and said, "Now I'm going to play it back and you can listen to everything you said." That was particularly interesting because they had never heard the sound of their own voices. They sat enthralled and I didn't have to delete a word. Jennie was astounded at their answers because she heard things about the old country, their families and lives that she had never heard before.

Years later I sat down with a recorder and computer to reduce the interviews to hard copy. I was shocked to realize

Jennie and Bob Briggs, 60th wedding anniversary, Thanksgiving 1998

that 30 years had passed since I made the recordings. Our folks had all passed away and there were their voices speaking to me once again.

When Jennie and I listen to the old recordings or read what they said, we are fascinated more by how their lives had influenced ours, than by the technological changes and standard of living that had occurred during theirs.

Without being aware of it, Jennie and I modeled our lives after theirs—marriage, a family, dedication to each other, family survival through the trials and tribulations of wars, depressions and illness. Being with each other, having fun together, seeing our progenies give rise to more progenies and then recognizing that they are our immortality.

Jennie and I respectfully submit brief stories and anecdotes that will serve to give you some glimpse of our parents, their lives and how they influenced ours. It is a pleasure having this opportunity to reminisce and once again reaffirm the importance of our parents in our lives.

A BRIEF HISTORY OF THE PARENTS OF
JANET (always Jennie) and ROBERT (always Bob) BRIGGS

Jennie's maternal grandmother, Janet Wilson of Scotland, married Arthur Cowan in 1876 and had 10 children, seven boys and three girls. Jennie's mother, Christine, the eldest girl, became a second mother to the family. Arthur died in 1906.

Jennie's paternal grandmother, Isabella of Scotland, married James in 1880 and had three boys. Jennie's father, David, the eldest boy, was 13 years old when his father died. As a means of providing family income, David was indentured to a brass manufacturing company to become a journeyman.

Christine lived in Airdrie, Scotland, and David lived a short distance away. David knew one of Christine's brothers but didn't know her. One day he saw him talking to her and later on asked if he knew the girl. The brother responded with, "Well, I ought to. She's my sister," and of course they were introduced and from that time on they were always "Teen and David."

Still teenagers, it wasn't long before they were making plans for their future. It was agreed that David would complete his training, become a journeyman, and go to America where he would work and save money to send for Teen.

The seven years completed, David was called into the office where he was presented his journeyman papers and told to report to the plant the next morning at the full pay of $1 per day. David accepted his papers, politely thanked them and said, "I won't be reporting to the plant because I'll be sailing to America on the *Sicilian*." He spent 10 days in steerage where he had a wonderful adventure, good food and landed in Halifax, Canada, in 1906.

He worked wherever jobs took him in Canada and the States and in 1910 he sent for Christine. She sailed first class to America on the *Columbia* and landed in New York City. They were married the next day in Nyack. Ultimately they settled in Detroit, Michigan, where he worked at the Cadillac Motor Car Company. Christine's mother, five brothers, both sisters, and many friends emigrated from Scotland and stayed with the Bruces until they found housing of their own. David's mother immigrated to Hamilton, Canada, where she stayed with friends. She occasionally visited David and Christine, but Canada was always home to her.

A Briggs from England arrived in America in 1680 and settled in Rhode Island. In 1776 five of the Briggs family served in the American Revolutionary Army. When it was over, Joseph Briggs went west and settled in Windsor, Ohio, where my grandfather, Alfred Briggs, was born. He served four years with the Third Ohio Infantry Regiment in the Civil War and was discharged in 1865. He met and married grandmother Lydia in Lansing, Michigan. They had two boys, Harry and Bernard. Grandfather Alfred died in 1902 and the boys were placed in a Grand Army of the Republic Orphanage in Dayton, Ohio, where they lived until they completed high school.

Jennie was 14 years old and I was 15 when we met at Woodland Beach, Michigan, on Lake Erie where our folks had summer cottages. From that summer on, it was always "Jennie

Mr. Briggs' paternal grandparents, 1864

and Bob." Jennie went to commercial college and worked while I went to Michigan State University. We married after I graduated as a civil engineer and followed projects around the country, eventually returning to Wyandotte, Michigan, and then Grosse Ile.

Our parents retired to Florida but occasionally returned to Michigan for brief visits. One summer when Jennie's folks were visiting us in Wyandotte, we were sitting in the back yard with our Scotty dog and David became annoyed at noisy children playing in the alley. He got up, went back and shouted over the fence for them to be quiet, then came back and sat down. Jennie's mother looked at him and said, "David, why do we have a dog if you're going to do all the barking?"

I stifled my laughter while David looked at me with sparkles in his eyes and said, "She is always saying things like that to me."

Until that moment I hadn't realized what a remarkable woman she was–intelligent, kind, quiet, reticent to speak up against anyone, never gossiped, had a wonderful sense of humor and was generous to a fault. If there ever was a Pollyanna, Christine Bruce was one. Everyone liked her, especially children–she was an ideal mother-in-law and grandmother.

When our children visited grandma, the first thing they'd say was, "Make us a cake, grandma," and she did. She never used a recipe and never a spoon. The children watched in fascination as she shook in flour, a gob of butter, little of this, a dob of that, a shake of salt, and pinches of various materials and finally a splash of milk. With the bowl in her lap she mixed the ingredients with vigor using the first two fingers of her right hand.

While the cake was baking, she made frosting the same way. That's when the children ran for slices of bread on which she spread gobs of frosting–with the first two fingers of her right hand. The diminished ingredients were replaced using the "little of this and that" technique. Her cakes and frostings were delicious.

It was said that back in Scotland, she read aloud to the family and she did the same in America to visiting sisters, brothers and families. One of our children once asked if she could draw a map of the United States. She proceeded to make a free-hand sketch, adding the states and their names.

Christine had the gift of perspicacity and could analyze a situation before you realized there was a problem. One time Jennie and I went shopping with her and the clerk was downright ornery and offensive. Christine said to the woman, "My-y-y you must be having a bad day."

The clerk stopped what she was doing, looked at mom for an instant, and tears flowed down her cheeks. Her voice trembled as she said, "Oh-h-h I have, everything has gone wrong today and you're the first person who understood." She dried her eyes with a tissue and said, "I feel better all ready." That was Christine–she always made you feel better.

After happy years in Florida, Christine and David became too old to live alone and Jennie and I brought them home to live with us on Grosse Ile. We lived together in gentle harmony and what we did–they did. They enjoyed having me play hymns on the organ and quietly sang or hummed along. Jennie often cooked dinners using mom's recipes that originated in Scotland. One was called "mintz" and consisted of ground meat, chopped onions, topped with sliced potatoes and simmered in a frying pan. It was popular back in Scotland because it was inexpensive and simple to prepare–important when cooking for a family of 12.

Jennie spiced it up, added a few more ingredients and created a delicious dinner. One time we had mintz and were having coffee and cake afterward when pa told Jennie how much he'd enjoyed the mintz. I said, "You know, mom, whenever I came home from college for a visit, you always served mintz." Mom kind of glowed at the recollection. Then I added, "But, you know, I didn't like it very much because it was so bland."

Right out of the blue, without thinking, David spoke up and said, "Neither did I."

Mom was absolutely flabbergasted and said, "Why I thought you liked it."

Pa knew he had blundered and didn't know what to say so he stood up, said, "Naw," and walked out of the room. Mom sat speechless, feeling hurt I'm sure, but typically didn't make an issue of it.

Consider: Mom had cooked mintz for Dave all their married life because she thought he liked it. Pa had eaten it all those years without complaining because he didn't want to hurt her feelings. That is true love.

David died three years before Christine. Both were 89 years old. They were cremated and laid to rest in the Memorial Garden of the Grosse Ile Presbyterian Church. They were born and raised on an island and rest to eternity on an island

EPILOGUE

The Book of Genesis in the Old Testament describes the creation of man in God's image. It tells that man was created from dust and placed in the Garden of Eden. God named the animals and then discovered he hadn't created a fitting mate for man and formed Eve from his rib.

The religion of the ancient Greeks describes a similar creation but a different version. God created man but not woman. God became so exasperated at man's outrageous acts that he cleaved man into two halves–thus creating man and woman. Ancient Greek philosophers believed this story and said that was why men and women were ever searching the world for their matching halves.

CHRISTINE and DAVID BRUCE
ELSIE and HARRY BRIGGS

They were abidingly faithful to each other, fully aware of their own strengths, weaknesses and peculiarities and those of their mates and accepted each other without hesitation or reluctance.

The matching halves were joined and became one and role models for their progenies.

Christine and David Bruce, Jennie's parents, 1967

Mrs. Margaret Parsons

"At an early age, I learned to appreciate the simple details in our home."

Reflecting on my life brings back many occasions and situations that I truly feel influenced my personal beliefs and attitudes. These experiences helped to develop my way of life and also assisted my children in their ability to make better decisions.

I grew up during the Depression when the banks crashed and everyone had to delve within themselves for resources to continue living. My parents were born into pioneering families, facing numerous challenges to exist. They were both from large families who had learned to share resources and responsibilities within their own households and, indeed, experienced many unique lessons.

At an early age, I learned to appreciate the simple details in our home. My mother used to let us watch her when she baked bread or when she prepared a cake or cookies for some very special occasion because she had to save sugar, only using it sparingly. She always saved bits of dough or ingredients for us to blend in our projects, relating stories of the grains they used to raise and have ground for flour. She sometimes shared with the Indians who would stop and ask for flour. She taught us to observe textures of each food to gauge the finished product.

My father used to entertain us in the evening before bedtime with stories he had heard and many experiences of his own youth, always with something we could glean for our own practical knowledge. He had a great repertoire of songs and stories. We felt blessed with knowledge and entertainment.

My parents had great faith in God and faithfully took us to church. We had few material things, yet felt blessed and enriched for the sharing of knowledge and love. I believe my children benefited from my background and learned to accept what we couldn't change, but appreciate what we did have.

When my children were very young, their father became critically ill and we had many years of severe circumstances to accept. The children bravely accepted it all, and had to help raise each other when their father did pass away. We value each other.

Mrs. Margaret Parsons, 1997

Mrs. Milka Puroff

"I think that in order to have a meaningful life, one needs to have others to give to and be needed by as well as to lean on for support."

I was born in Toledo, Ohio, on November 22, 1928. We were raised in a very tightly knit immigrant community on the east side of the city. My father, a self-made businessman, made sure we had the best of everything. Because of his distrust of banking institutions, we were never touched by the financial plights of other families during the Depression.

We traveled abroad, took dance and horseback riding lessons and our mother saw to it that we (the girls) were proficient as cooks and housekeepers. All in all, we were a typical first-generation 1930s family of comfortable means.

Not surprisingly, my feelings on the important things in life also center around the family. I was raised to become a dutiful daughter, wife and mother, and to this end I have given it my utmost. I married at age 26 and raised three daughters, all successful and accomplished young women. I believe helping my children is and always will be my first priority in life. My most important aspect of existence is my family. After losing my husband to cancer, my friendships with others, especially other widows, have deepened and developed into a (as my daughters jokingly refer to it) "Widow Brigade!!" We have so much in common and it's a comfort to know I can talk and relate to

Mrs. Milka Puroff as child with aunts and mother, Greece, 1932

someone who shares the feelings and situations widowed senior citizens are faced with in daily life.

My church and community work are third in my hierarchy of importance in my life. To this I commit many hours in the capacity of church board member as well as president of my seniors club.

I think that in order to have a meaningful life, one needs to have others to give to and be needed by as well as to lean on for support. Without the love and support of family and friends, one's life would be sad, empty and meaningless. The give and take of family and friendships is, in my opinion, what a fulfilling life is all about.

❖

Mr. Clyde Picard

*"While in the service, my brother, Dr. Joseph Picard,
constantly encouraged me to seek a college education. . . .
This was the turning point in my life."*

I was raised in the blue-collar community of east Dearborn,
Michigan. While in high school, a college education was not a
top priority. I decided to pursue an industrial curriculum with a
major in electricity.

When I graduated from high school, I worked in several facto-
ries. The Army was still drafting as a result of World War II, so
three of us joined the Army for three years instead of waiting to
be drafted for two years. While in the service, my brother, Dr.
Joseph Picard, constantly encouraged me to seek a college education. After a couple of years in the service, I agreed that if the
government gave the Korean War veterans the GI Bill, I would
attend college. They did, so I went to college.

This was the turning point in my life. I had taken an instructor course in the Army and decided to seek a career in education.
My goal in life became teaching, helping, and coaching young
people in a local high school.

I taught mathematics and coached for 39 years. This life
endeavor was the most rewarding of careers. My wife, Evelyn,
helped me finish college while working and having our first
child. She also is a believer in education and encouraged our
children to attend college. We have nine children and eight of

them have college degrees. The ninth child has two years of college and today is a successful businessman.

I would like to thank my brother for encouraging me to continue my education. Most of all, I would like to thank my wife for her love and support.

Mr. Clyde Picard, 1995

Mr. Tom Moore

"I have found that if you work hard, play hard and observe the Golden Rule, life will be worth living."

I was born in a small town near Glasgow, Scotland, in the midst of World War I. My father worked in the local steel mill and we often heard stories about the blackouts and bomb scares.

When I was a young boy, we came to the United States. My father preceded us and found employment. He then sent for the rest of us—my mother, two sisters and me. I vividly remember when I started school how my classmates would giggle when I was called upon to recite. They liked to hear my accent. I did quite well in the new schools and graduated as the president of my high school class.

The economy at this time was very slow and I had to go to work to help the family. My first job was for the YMCA as a bookkeeper, clerk and telephone switchboard operator. I worked afternoons and on the opposite side of town. A few years later, the "Y" suggested that I look for a new job (on their time), because I could not progress any further there. I then found a job as a hotel auditor and soon thereafter married my high school sweetheart.

World War II broke out and I enlisted as a cadet in the Air Corps. When I graduated, I was retained as an instructor to teach cadets Bombardiering and Navigation. When the war

*Tom and Hilda Moore, 60th wedding anniversary,
1998–a milestone they attribute to a philosophy of
"being respectful of each other"*

was coming to a close we adopted a baby girl, Gayle, and were
soon on our way home. The three of us were then sent to Buffalo,
New York, where I was the resident auditor. When I returned to
Detroit a few years later, my employers had started to buy various hotels and office buildings in the eastern Midwest. I was
then made a traveling auditor and visited these properties once
each month. This meant that I was away from home five days
each week. The weekends were iffy when the winter storms
snarled my transportation. During this period we adopted a
baby boy, Robert, and I continued to work until my retirement–
a total of 42 years with the same organization.

I am very grateful to my family for the love and support they gave me while I was away from home. I am very proud to say my Army wife and I just recently celebrated our 60th wedding anniversary. Even though our family was not always together during the week, we had a strong faith and always made it a point to go to church every Sunday, not only to worship, but to take an active part in various activities. I served as church treasurer for 33 years.

Life has not always been easy. I felt cheated that I had not experienced the day-to-day progress of our children. My wife, Hilda, had to be a Girl and Boy Scout leader and also the everyday electrician, plumber and jack-of-all-trades. We lost our newly married son, a Detroit policeman who was killed in the line of duty. I then had open-heart surgery and five years ago my wife suffered a stroke that left her partially paralyzed on the left side. I have found that if you work hard, play hard and observe the Golden Rule, life will be worth living.

❖

Mrs. Lorene Temple

"Her butter was the prettiest I have ever seen."

I believe my outlook on life was formed from both my Christian faith and my early years of life. I was born in Louisiana to parents who were very poor sharecroppers. I learned to work at an early age in the fields picking cotton. My mother died in 1929 at the age of 26. I was almost 7 years old, my sister 4 years, and my little brother lacked five days of being 1 year old.

Our paternal grandparents took us in and, from her bed, my grandmother taught me how to cook. She was ill with cancer. When you have to grow up at the age of 7, you learn a lot very quickly. Anything anyone did for us was a great treat, like giving us food or hand-me-down clothes. You quickly learn the value of food and having a few clothes and are also thankful to God for taking care of your needs.

I will always remember how I enjoyed the foods of two special people—one was my maternal grandmother. We always looked forward to going to her home and spending the night. She could not take care of us when my mother died because five of her nine children were still at home. My grandmother could make the best hot oatmeal in the world. There wasn't any "quick" or "instant" in those days. She would make a big pot of oatmeal and we would all line up on the long wooden benches on each side of the long crude homemade table. She would dish us our oatmeal and we would put sugar and whole milk on it. Our milk at home was skimmed because we had to have the cream to churn in a hand crock for a little butter. To this day I dislike skimmed milk.

The other person was Aunt Mary. Aunt Mary lived about half way between our house and where we walked three miles each way to school. She would see us coming home from school and, in the winter when we were very cold, she would call us in and give us homemade sugar cookies and butter. Her butter was the prettiest I have ever seen. It was very yellow and she would mold it in a wooden butter-mold press, and it would have a beautiful rose imprinted on top. Until she died, when I went back to my home in the South, I would visit Aunt Mary. We really loved each other.

When you have to move so much as sharecroppers (I counted 21 times once), it is very hard in school. We moved just as my grade was about to start to learn fractions. Arithmetic was one of my favorite subjects. When I went to the new school they were into fractions and, because I didn't get the basic beginning, I was having a terrible time and in tears. We, however, had a neighbor who was a well-educated man. One day I asked him if he knew how to do fractions. This blessed man came to teach me and when he left I was so happy because he had taught me how to do fractions. This opened me up like sunshine. Needless to say, I didn't have any more problems with fractions and, to this day, I am eternally grateful to this man.

We had good schoolteachers. Our teachers were treated with respect, and it was an honor to be a teacher in those days. I believe if there were more love and respect in our world, it would be a much better place in which to live. To me, Dr. Ulrich and Dr. Waldinger are good examples for us all to follow.

My outlook on life is reflected in my own family life. We are a closely knit family. A family reunion is held every Labor Day weekend, and 35 or 40 of us celebrate Thanksgiving, Christmas and the New Year together. We love each other, and there is no backbiting. We always end our day by making music, singing and giving thanks to God. Our children have grown up in this tradition and I pray they will continue after we are gone. I firmly believe the family is the backbone of our nation and our world.

I think from this little writing you can tell I love life and the Master Craftsman who gave it to me. Each new day is a challenge and it's up to us to do our best.

Mrs. Lorene Temple and daughter Carol, Mother's Day, 1988

Anonymous Patient

"So my son and I had three surprises wrapped into this one game."

What is my philosophy? Quite simple stated, it is the conscious effort and practice to implement two age-old adages with a focus on the development of strong values. We have all heard or read (1) a family that plays together and prays together stays together, and (2) do unto others as you would want them to do unto you. Practice family unity and live, eat and play together.

An example of togetherness in my immediate family can be exemplified in going back to the early years of married life when my two sons were in elementary school. They became very interested in participating in the T-ball league that was sponsored as part of the local youth recreation program. This interest may have been a "rub-off" of dad's interest in sports and athletics in general.

At the time of my sons' participation in T-ball, it became commonplace for the three of us to play and practice in our backyard. This was a natural outgrowth of "playing together and being together" in its early stages. When years had gone by (the older son became 11 years of age and the younger son was approaching 8), the Detroit Tigers won the American League baseball title and then played the National League team and won the 1968 World Series.

The early practice of playing together in their T-ball years helped peak their interest to attend a World Series game at Tiger Stadium. Naturally, tickets were hard to procure by the ordinary fan. However, the Tiger organization conducted a lottery drawing of names for interested fans who filed and paid for entry into the lottery drawing.

Luckily, I "won" the opportunity to purchase two tickets to an assigned game in the series. On the day of the scheduled game, it was my misfortune to have been sent out of town on a business trip. In my absence on the day of the game, my wife and older son went to the game thus fulfilling his high expectations of personally viewing the Detroit Tigers in action. This incident focuses on the adage—a family that plays together stays together.

As luck would have it, later in the series I was fortunate to have been given two box-seat tickets to a second game. These two seats were to the left side of the Tiger dugout on the third base side of the field, giving us an open and close-up view of all the players. And then, a short time prior to the start of the game, a gentleman was ushered to our box seat location and we three began to converse. A surprise to me, and especially to my 11-year-old son, this gentleman was #01 Casey Stengel, who was known to all baseball fans. He has since been immortalized in the annals of baseball lore. For another surprise that same day, the first baseball (a ceremonial pitch) was thrown by the legendary Hubert Humphrey. So my son and I had three surprises wrapped into this one game:

1. Gratis box seat tickets to a World Series game.
2. Meeting and sitting in the box with Casey Stengel.
3. Observing Senator Humphrey (Democrat, Minnesota) throw out the ceremonial baseball.

In a brief summary again, with father and son in attendance at the World Series game, the saying goes, "The family that plays together will usually stay together."

Another memorable experience of the family "playing" together came about several years later and prior to my retirement. To revert a bit to my days of employment, I had received an invitation from the Goodyear management to ride on the Goodyear blimp when it was in the southeast Michigan area to fly over the Pontiac Silverdome during a televised NFL Monday Night football game. After having accepted the invitation for the ride, I met with a schedule conflict that compelled me to cancel the ride. I related this missed opportunity to my family as the years went by.

However, having missed the first opportunity, I was elated when I received a second chance in December 1996. This time the ride was in California when my younger son was instrumental and able to schedule a blimp ride for four of the family—my son, his wife, their 1-year-old daughter, and yours truly. The ride took us over the Los Angeles area and the nearby coastline.

Having missed the first opportunity to fly on the blimp, I wanted to capitalize on the second. It was a beautiful California-type day with a blue sky and fluffy white clouds. As I sat in the copilot seat, I was able to converse quite extensively with the pilot who was most gracious in providing flight data and suggested sights to observe. For example, the blimp can seat five passengers on each flight due to very limited space. We "floated" at 30 to 35 mph at an altitude of approximately 3,000 to 3,500 feet, although I was told that the blimp is capable to attain an altitude of approximately 10,000 feet.

Moreover, all the current Goodyear airships are equipped with a network of colored lights attached to their sides to flash messages after dark. The night sign on the blimp that I rode was called the *Super Skytacular* and was 105 feet long and 24.5 feet high. From the Rose Bowl to the Indy 500 races, and from the U.S. Open golf tournament to the Statue of Liberty's 100th birthday party, the Goodyear blimps have covered it all as an advertising medium and the aerial eyes of a television viewing audience.

Again, a truly unusual experience was to have this sightseeing flight on the blimp. I considered this second opportunity and the arrangement executed by my son to be an outgrowth of the family efforts to promulgate family value. Leisure-time fun as a family unit? Yes! Play, have fun and stay together!

FINIS . . . My philosophy of life is spelled in one capitalized word and that word is "FAMILY"!

Commentary:

In the early years of my practice, I coached several sports for my children while they were in elementary school. This often meant significant schedule changes during the particular coaching season. I was always impressed that my patients not only supported my efforts to coach, but encouraged them, despite the inconvenience of changing office hours and rescheduling appointments. I thank these patients for their support and recognition of the importance of family time.

The efforts we make on behalf of our children are returned at a later time. My children have already given so much to me.

To My Children

Dear Jason,

The day you were born I looked into your eyes and you had this great smile on your face. Everything that is wonderful and good in the world, I saw at that moment and continue to see in you every day. I admire your honesty and integrity.

In your life, you will have challenges to overcome. It is your response to these challenges that is important. Faith, love, humor, acceptance, forgiveness and compassion are some of the tools God has given you to aid you in your time of need and in your response.

Mom and I will always be there for you as well. The following blessing, given to me by a friend, has great meaning to me:

"I pray that you will be
strong in trial,
wise in confusion,
calm in chaos, and
abounding in love.

May others look to you for
understanding when troubled,
hope when tested,
courage when frightened, and
a brother when alone.

May God bless all of your coming
and goings,
May He bless every life you touch.
May He bless your accomplishments
and fulfill your dreams.
And, at the end of each day,
may you rest with the assurance
that you have been a
good and faithful servant.

May God bless you today and always."

Happy Birthday.

Love,
Dad

Beyond Imagination

To My Son, Jason

Hello, my son
You've just been born
With you in my arms
A new life begins.

Beyond imagination
Wondrous celebration
With you in my arms
A new life begins.

Everything good
And wonderful
In this world
I see at this moment
Peaceful sensation
Beyond imagination
Wondrous celebration.

The first day of school
Mom watches her little boy
Tear on her cheek
Heart pounding
The world awaits
You are the one
My only son.

The light in your room
Calls me in the evening
Nighttime stories
Baseball glories
You are the one
My only son.

You be the ball
I'll be the glove
Your hand in mine

We move in time
Forever is my love
Like the Heavens above.

I'm looking up at you now
Everything good and wonderful I see
Every day, every moment
Beyond imagination
Wondrous celebration
Peaceful sensation.

You be the ball
I'll be the glove
Your hand in mine
We move in time
Forever is my love
Like the Heavens above.

T.P.W.

Jason Waldinger with father, Dr. Thomas Waldinger,
Windemere Park, Ann Arbor, Michigan, 1988

Dear Emily,

There are qualities about you that are remarkable. Whenever we spend time together or talk, you make me feel better. That's a gift. I have also noticed that you share this attribute with family, your friends and people you meet. This is important because it has a positive effect on those around you.

Other special qualities you have are the joy, laughter, sense of humor and sparkle that you bring to each day. It's fun and exciting to be your father.

I admire your sensitivity and caring for family and friends. You always have a genuine interest in others. Your Grandpa Herman once told me that truly remarkable people do things for others when it is not convenient or when it may be difficult for them. You have shared that trait with me many times.

One of my greatest joys is seeing these remarkable qualities in you and knowing that you will accomplish great things in the future. Carl Sandburg wrote the following poem. It reflects my feelings about you:

> ". . .I love you for what you are
> knowing so well what you are.
> And I love you more yet, child,
> deeper yet than ever, child,
> for what you are going to be,
> knowing so well you are going far,
> knowing your great works are ahead,
> ahead and beyond,
> yonder and far over yet."

Happy Birthday.

Love,
Dad

Forever and Always

To My Daughter, Emily

Smiles and kisses
Eyes that sparkle
Hugs that caress my soul
Greetings at home
Never alone
The one who makes me whole.

Smiles and kisses
Blueberry Buckle
Stars that paint the sky
Forever and always
In this world
My little girl.

The moment I see you
My heart soars
I am forever yours
Walks in the park
Talks after dark
My little girl.

You take me places
I've never been
The world opens its arms
Your hand in mine
We move in time
Forever my little girl.

The moment I see you
My heart soars
I am forever yours
Forever and always
In this world
My little girl.

T.P.W.

Emily Waldinger, Leland, Michigan, 1989

Mrs. Leila Hayes

"My life has been a combination of joy and sorrow, but the joys have far outnumbered the latter."

Life is a journey. It is up to us to make the most of it. We have all the wonderful things God gave us–the sky, the earth and the seas that surround us. All we have to do is live our lives as if every day is the last.

There are ups and downs along the way, but we accept them and go on. We become aware of others, our brothers and sisters regardless of race or creed.

My life has been a combination of joy and sorrow, but the joys have far outnumbered the latter. In my 96 years I have lived to see many wonderful inventions and great progress in medical science. I am thankful to God for everything.

Mrs. Leila Hayes, 1986 - now 96 years of age

Commentary:

It is an honor to have you as a patient and be a small part in your life's journey.

"Youth is not a time of life–it is a state of mind. It is not a matter of red cheeks, red lips and supple knees. It is a temper of the will; a quality of the imagination; a vigor of the emotions; it is the freshness of the deep springs of life. Youth means a temperamental predominance of courage over timidity, of the appetite for adventure over the love of ease. This often exists in a man of fifty, more than a boy of twenty. Nobody grows old by merely living a number of years; people grow old by deserting their ideals.

"Years may wrinkle the skin, but to give up enthusiasm wrinkles the soul. Worry, doubt, self-distrust, fear and despair–these are the long, long years that bow the head and turn the growing spirit back to dust.

"Whether seventy or sixteen, there is in every being's heart a love of wonder; the sweet amazement at the stars and starlike things and thoughts; the undaunted challenge of events, the unfailing, childlike appetite for what comes next, and the joy in the game of life.

"You are as young as your faith, as old as your doubt; as young as your self-confidence, as old as your fear, as young as your hope, as old as your despair.

"In the central place of your heart there is a wireless station. So as long as it receives messages of beauty, hope, cheer, grandeur, courage, and power from the earth, from men and from the Infinite–so long are you young. When the wires are all down and the central places of your heart are covered with the snows of pessimism and ice of cynicism, then are you grown old, indeed!"

– Samuel Ullman

❖

Mrs. Gretchen Matucha

"He has been an inspiration to our whole family."

Many events in my life have had a profound effect on the person I have become and how I face life. When I was born, my parents were Iowa farmers. They made so much of the little they had, but always found time and ways to help their family.

I met my husband, Raymond, in high school and we were married in Iowa. Shortly thereafter, he took a job in Chicago and I had to travel there alone. He began his career with a large corporation in the mail-sorting department and worked his way up in management to a supervisory position. Money was very tight starting out and he only had a high school education plus a few night school classes. I so admired the way he worked for his family and provided a comfortable home and college education for our three children. We lived in a small, five-room apartment for 20 years, but they were some of the happiest days of my life.

Two months before he was to retire, my husband was diagnosed with cancer. It required surgery and the Christmas holidays were approaching. Our children and two little grandchildren went to the hospital that Christmas Eve. It seemed to draw us all closer together. His positive attitude toward this disease kept all of us going. He also has undergone heart-valve surgery

Gretchen and Raymond Matucha, 1993

and has severe arthritis in his back, which causes him to rely on a wheelchair these days when leaving our home. With all of these ailments, I have seldom if ever heard him complain about how he feels. He has been an inspiration to our whole family.

Today we live in a retirement community. Most evenings we have dinner with a couple I greatly admire. After a very active life, the wife suffered a stroke in her early 60s. She is only able to speak a couple of words and is confined to a wheelchair, but she always has a smile and a wonderful sense of humor, which is displayed by her hearty laugh. Her devoted husband is always there for her and they enjoy kidding each other in their own special way. They have also been an inspiration to me.

After 63 years of marriage, our family now includes three children, six grandchildren and six great-grandchildren. Sharing time with all of them and watching their families grow are my inspiration today. My church and religion also give me the strength I need. I feel that I have been blessed in many ways during my lifetime.

Commentary:

During my first year of practice, I was asked to give a lecture on skin cancer to senior citizens at Oakwood Hospital. Because my main interest in dermatology is skin cancer and geriatric dermatology, I readily accepted. However, in the middle of my lecture, the slide projector malfunctioned. A senior citizen quickly came to my aid, namely, Mr. Matucha. He fixed the projector and I was able to complete my presentation. His help was greatly appreciated.

Both Mr. and Mrs. Matucha became patients of mine. I have enjoyed seeing them and their graciousness has only increased. Two years ago, Mrs. Matucha called me at home on a Saturday with a dermatological concern. Although she only wanted me to provide assistance over the phone, I insisted on coming to the office to see her. I was happy to have the opportunity to repay the kindness Mr. Matucha had extended to me 14 years ago at Oakwood Hospital.

Mrs. Matucha writes that her parents always found time to help and that Mr. Matucha is an inspiration to their family. I appreciate the help Mr. Matucha gave me in the first year of my practice. Mr. Matucha, you are an inspiration to me as well.

Mrs. Amelia Rutila

"I loved every day of it."

The greatest influence in my life was my parents. They were Finnish immigrants who came to America to better their lives. My father came here at the age of 17, because he would have otherwise been taken into the Russian Army. I wish I knew more about his life and his coming to Canada and then moving to the Upper Peninsula of Michigan. He worked in the copper mines and eventually became a farmer. After farming, he became an insurance agent.

In the meantime, he learned the English language with the help of my sisters and brothers. He believed so strongly in education that it was instilled in all of us. I remember when my oldest sister came home, books and all, and said she quit school. She knew better because she went back the next day, finished high school, and became a teacher, like my three other sisters and I.

Mother came to America as an indentured servant. She had worked for a Lutheran minister who paid her way so she could come to this country. She was a quiet soul who believed in helping those in need. I remember when we had a terrible flu epidemic in this country. Homes were quarantined and families were in desperate need of help and food. Mother was always

Mrs. Amelia Rutila, 1924

ready to help. She waited until the dark of night before she would go to help her neighbors with food and homemade loaves of bread. We as children worried that she might be seen and would be reported to the authorities. She always said, "You can't let human beings suffer."

It was a coincidence that my first teaching job was in the south end of Dearborn at the Salina School. My students were immigrants whose parents came from many European countries. I couldn't begin to name all the nationalities because there were so many. I guess my own background helped these children with their difficulties. It was rewarding for me to spend my 38 years in the same school. Education was so important to these students, like mine was in the far north of Michigan.

Having had so many experiences, I'll just mention what happened to me a few weeks ago. I was in the grocery store and this woman came up to me and said, "You are Mrs. Rutila. Do you remember me?" I had to look closely at her and then a bell rang! "You are Lena Carpalango." Lena had won a spelling bee on one Friday. We had a spelling bee every Friday. The students knew I would always reward them with something. She got a Hershey bar and was so delighted because she had never had a candy bar. She came from a family of 12. Most of the families in the area were large, and they had very little.

Another student heard I was at the Salina School 75th Anniversary and she wrote to me from Florida and reminded me that she still had the dictionary that she received after winning a spelling bee. Sometime I will tell you about the doctor I met who recognized me. I taught him in the third grade in 1939!

Teaching was my mission in life. What more can I say at the age of 92. I loved every day of it.

Commentary:

Mrs. Rutila writes that her mother was a great soul who believed in helping others in need. She always said, "You can't let human beings suffer." I know that Mrs. Rutila incorporated these philosophies throughout her life and in her mission in life—teaching. You are an extraordinary person.

Your philosophy of life statement reflects the kind and compassionate words of Mother Teresa to the poor, homeless and infirm: "May we be worthy to serve you."

❖

Mrs. Betty Szekely

"Don't complain and remember you can do anything if you sincerely try."

By the examples my father gave me to follow and his explanations of how to adjust to problems, my moral and religious values and attitudes were formed. My father helped me to adjust smoothly to the outside world. He inculcated in me two ideas that have helped me through life: Don't complain and remember you can do anything if you sincerely try.

My father and I spent a great deal of time together fishing. His insightful discussions with me as we sat in the rowboat were more meaningful than any sociology or psychology class that I was ever enrolled in. He early on taught me how to mediate disputes with my parents, peers, relatives and neighbors. By example, I was shown that there are other alternatives in all disputes. It is a waste of time to blame others for our problems. In other words, don't complain. Many conflicts in our lives could be brought to a quick conclusion if we would search our hearts for alternatives and not be prideful. Instead of complaining, my father told me that if I tried to be kind, cheerful and considerate to others, my heart would be able to handle life's catastrophes. During his life, he showed me daily the above moral qualities and they always seemed to work for him, thus the more reason for me to emulate him.

Because it was always his suggestion that I could succeed in any endeavor if I tried, after staying home and raising my two sons, I began college at the age of 40. Never did it occur to me that I couldn't do it. My goal was a college degree from the University of Michigan. I shared this goal through the years during office visits with Dr. Ulrich. He also supported my goal. In fact, Dr. Ulrich and my father were both tremendous counselors. How frightened I was that first day of college, yet I never doubted that I could do it. Three years later, I received my degree from the University of Michigan, proof you can obtain your goals if you sincerely try.

Recently, I found a wall plaque with the following verse:

> "Lord, help me remember that nothing is going to happen today that YOU and I can't handle."

The teachings of my father, the love of my Lord and the above verse get me through each day. What a great and wondrous life I have had.

Commentary:

Mrs. Szekely shared with me her memories of fishing with her father and the profound influence he had on her life. I told Mrs. Szekely of my daughter's love of fishing and of our fishing expeditions.

You have not only had a wondrous life, but your wisdom is wondrous as well. Perhaps some day, you and Emily can fish together, and you can share your wisdom with her.

Mr. Edward Fritz

"I could continue with my hobby as usual with my best fishing partner–my wife, Jozefa."

In 1983, I began my long delayed retirement. For nearly four decades as an avid fisherman, I enjoyed the warmth and the beauty of bright sunny days. Very little was said about too much sunlight. A good "glow" was expected after a weekend fishing. Being a blond, fair-skinned fisherman, I often came home with a bit more than just a light tan on my skin. A hat? Well, I did not think it was that important. As the years passed, I noticed that blotches started appearing on my face and hands. These lesions failed to heal easily. On the advice of my family physician, I was referred to a dermatologist, Dr. Waldinger. His diagnosis of skin cancer was terrifying. I thought that after surviving WWII and the camps, the hunger and the abuse, this would have been a lousy way to finish my life.

What a relief it was when I was told that mine was probably the most readily treated form of skin cancer. As the treatments started and were continued, the blotches reduced in number. Am I free of them? No, unfortunately. I did permanent damage to my skin so they probably will keep recurring, but they can be held in check.

Did I give up fishing? You have got to be kidding! With proper protection I could continue with my hobby as usual with my best fishing partner–my wife, Jozefa. When she passed away in 1995, I thought my world had collapsed. During that time, I can remember especially the kind gesture of coffee and a snack from Dr. Waldinger when I visited him for my regular checkups. It is this kind of "medicine" that should be complimented–a medicine that tends to the spirit as well as to the body. Thank you, Doctor.

Mr. Edward Fritz, Dearborn, Michigan, April 1999

Commentary:

Thank you so much for your kind words. You are a delight and a joy to see. Every book needs at least two fishing stories. You have made my book complete.

FISHING

"When the wind is in the East,
Then the fishes bite the least;
When the wind is in the West,
Then the fishes bite the best;
When the wind is in the North,
Then the fishes do come forth;
When the wind is in the South,
It blows the bait in the fish's mouth."

– Anonymous

❖

Mrs. Shirley Stephens

"I learned from my parents about being kind and helping others."

I often wonder why God has blessed me with such a good life. I was born in 1925 to loving parents and had a great childhood in a religious home. I attended Catholic schools for 12 years. My parents were very generous people and were always helping others.

My grandmother came to live with us when she couldn't be by herself anymore. We would also have a lady friend from a nursing home over for dinner once a week. Anytime someone dropped in for a visit, my mother would put the teakettle on and we would sit around the kitchen table and have tea and toast. I learned from my parents about being kind and helping others.

I cared for both my father and mother before they died, and also an aunt who had no one close. They all set a good example for me.

My mother was a great letter writer. If we were away at camp, school or on vacation, one would always receive a letter from her. When she died, I inherited her writing desk and I'm now busy writing at least three letters a week. Moreover, I send many greeting cards to family and friends. Everyone enjoys hearing from me and keeping in touch.

I married a great man in May 1948 and have four wonderful children, their spouses and seven grandchildren. They are all so caring and concerned about us. Albert and I celebrated our 50th wedding anniversary in May and our family all got together and gave us a great party. It was wonderful being together with family and friends.

I've had some crises in my life, but God has always answered my prayers and things have worked out. I don't know what the future holds but I'll just keep my faith in God and He will see me through. He always has.

Commentary:

"I don't know what the future holds but I'll just keep my faith in God and He will see me through."

– Mrs. Shirley Stephens

And the Lord went before them by day in a pillar of cloud, to lead them the way; and by night in a pillar of fire, to give them light that they might go by day and by night: the pillar of cloud by day, and the pillar of fire by night, departed not from before the people.

– Exodus 13:21

Shirley and Albert Stephens, wedding day, 1948

Mr. Earl Lewis

*"When my three children were growing up, I made it a
point never to be too busy to answer their questions."*

I was born in Cumberland, Maryland, in August of 1922. This
is a small city in western Maryland in rather a scenic, moun-
tainous country. I was an only child but had lots of cousins.

In 1942, I enlisted in the U.S. Army and was in the southwest
Pacific Operations, namely New Guinea and the Philippine
campaigns from October 1942 to October 1945. It was then
when I realized how important life is, especially with death
hovering all around.

I suppose it was through these experiences that I decided I
was going to have an attitude of "It is better to be nice to people.
A smile or a pleasant word is not that difficult."

When my three children were growing up, I made it a point
never to be too busy to answer their questions. If I did not know
the answer, I would search around until I did. I remember one
time a group of us were at a friend's house talking and socializ-
ing, when his youngest son ran in the room and tried to get his
dad's attention. Well, the father ignored the son and sent him
away. Shortly after that, his oldest son came in the room and
told his dad that a room in the house was on fire! If the father
had listened, the damage would not have been nearly as bad.

The last item was when my wife, Jacqueline, was terminally ill with lung and bone cancer in the early 1990s. This lady suffered terribly, but never complained. Then one night she said, "I wish I would go to sleep and never wake up." That was her gentle way of saying, "I have had enough." She was more concerned about me attending to her than her problem.

Commentary:

You have shared so many smiles with me in the office. I cannot tell you how much this has meant. Your inherent kindness and goodness are always felt.

Mr. Earl Lewis, 1980

Mr. Don Boughner

"My belief in God's caring hand in all things has been a strength to me and will continue to be that for which I daily give thanks."

On my faith journey through life, as a child, son, college student, church member, soldier in the Army in Korea, friend, neighbor and teacher, I have observed the universality of good and evil. My mother was a friend to all she knew and was always there when her care was needed. It has been my good fortune to have had good examples in my life, whether they attended church as I did or not. My belief in God's caring hand in all things has been a strength to me and will continue to be that for which I daily give thanks. Therefore, I feel the need daily also to reach out to someone with a hurt or need, and to let them know by word or deed that I care for them, giving help or encouragement, as I am able.

Commentary:

> "Try not to become a man of success,
> but rather try to become a man of value."

> – Albert Einstein

Mrs. Doris Cherry

"Live, love, listen and forgive is my philosophy."

A very good friend of mine became estranged from her father and stopped talking to him. One day she decided to talk to me regarding this situation. She had to decide whether to leave it as is, or try to rectify it. I had tried in the past to show her the futility of leaving it as it is, but she refused to listen.

This time I finally got through to her and convinced her that life was too short for this kind of behavior. I told her that she would feel so much better if she could just forget the past and make up with her father and forgive him for whatever it was he was supposed to have done.

It took her a little time but she was finally able to forgive but not forget. About six months later, her father passed away. She came to me and thanked me for giving her those last six months with her father.

Listen and don't give advice unless it is asked for. Live, love, listen and forgive is my philosophy. We are thankful to God every day for all His blessings.

Commentary:

". . .Forgiveness is the means for taking what is broken and making it whole. It takes our broken hearts and mends them. It takes our trapped hearts and frees them. It takes our hearts blemished with shame and guilt and returns them to their unspoiled state once again. Forgiveness restores our hearts to the innocence that we once knew–an innocence that allowed us the freedom to love.

"When we forgive and are forgiven, our lives are always transformed. The sweet promises of forgiveness are kept. And we are actually given a fresh start with ourselves and the world."

– Robin Casarjian

Mr. & Mrs. Charles Jabour

"Our philosophy is to love and respect others, accepting their strengths, weaknesses and beliefs, whether they are family, friends, or new acquaintances."

We have been married for 52 years and have 10 children, 25 grandchildren and one great-grandson.

We have always been a closely knit family, communicating on a regular basis even though many live a great distance away. As difficult as it has been at times, all of us have managed to get together at the same time at least once or twice a year, plus individual visits. The recent death of our daughter-in-law at an early age has brought our family even closer together. All attended her funeral. She put up a valiant fight and hardly complained and was an inspiration to all of us.

Our philosophy is to love and respect others, accepting their strengths, weaknesses and beliefs, whether they are family, friends, or new acquaintances. We feel the best way to teach this is through example. Our children and their families have made us feel that their philosophies are similar to ours.

After we are gone, it is our prayer that their love and respect for each other will endure.

Commentary:

Mr. and Mrs. Charles Jabour have taught me the importance of acceptance by example.

> I asked God for strength that I might achieve.
> I was made weak that I might learn humbly to obey.
> I asked for health that I might do greater things.
> I was given infirmity that I might do better things.
> I asked for riches that I might be happy.
> I was given poverty that I might be wise.
> I asked for power that I might have the praise of men.
> I was given weakness that I might feel the need of God.
> I asked for all things that I might enjoy life.
> I was given life that I might enjoy all things.
> I got nothing that I asked for, but everything I had hoped for.
> Almost despite myself, my unspoken prayers were answered.
> I am, among all men, most richly blessed.

– The Prayer of an Unknown Confederate Soldier

Rose Marie and Charles Jabour, 50th wedding anniversary, 1996

Dr. James Rynearson

"One of His Boys"

I would like to share with you an incident of many years ago when two professionally trained men willingly shared their insight and encouragement with a most personable and academically talented young collegiate male.

The year is 1941 and in Ypsilanti, the then Michigan State Normal College had been preparing embryonic teachers for almost a century. One such student was a senior by the name of Victor Apple, who was majoring in physical education. This student's advisor was my father, Professor Elton J. Rynearson, who also served as athletic director and football coach and taught Anatomy and Physiology.

Elton Rynearson enjoyed his association with these young men and particularly those who participated on the college athletic teams. He followed closely "His Boys" as they went out into the world to provide their contributions. No doubt such a reward surely would have awaited Victor Apple had it not been for an unfortunate, or perhaps fortunate, injury to his knee during his senior year of collegiate football.

Immediately, Professor Rynearson contacted Dr. Carl Badgely of the Orthopedic Department at the University of Michigan Hospital. He had always been so considerate of the Ypsilanti college's needs, and he once again rendered his service. The diagnosis revealed an avulsion of the knee known as Osgood-Schlatter's disease. The necessary surgery was performed and the injury was basically corrected.

However, the story does not end there. So impressed by Dr. Badgely's skills, duties and good will, Victor Apple qualified for and graduated from the University of Michigan Medical School and served as Dr. Badgely's Chief Assistant. In his office on the ground level of the old University Hospital, Dr. Badgely placed a picture of Victor Apple on the wall reserved for "His Boys."

Commentary:

"The divine guidance often comes when the horizon is the blackest."

– Mohandas Karamchand (Mahatma) Gandhi

Dr. James Rynearson, 1973

Mrs. Helen Bandyke

"I have found to live well is to work well."

Due to family circumstances, I grew up fast. My first job after a lot of fruitless searching was in a mental hospital. Some of you might remember St. Joseph's Retreat at Michigan Avenue and Outer Drive in Dearborn, Michigan. I was only 18 years old at the time. The experience at first was frightening but, with time, the most gratifying job I ever had. I found that kindness works all the time. Even the most disturbed patients responded. Sister Julianna, a Sister of Charity, was my superior and also my surrogate mother. I had lost my own mother when I was 15.

I have found to live well is to work well. During World War II, I worked on the B-29 planes while my husband was in the service. It filled my time and I felt I was helping the war effort. I met lovely people. One was most special and she became my first child's godmother. I have three children; all are serious, hard-working individuals. My son is on public radio, one daughter is a teacher, and my older daughter is a supervisor at Ford Motor Company.

At the age of 77, I have been in the optical field for 37 years. Each working day gives me an opportunity to do good in many ways. I listen to people and their problems, and extend some kindness. Moreover, I am doing myself a favor by being involved and keeping my mind active.

Commentary:

Mrs. Helen Bandyke exhibits a wonderful resilience. In his book, *Values of the Game*, Bill Bradley writes:

". . .Resilience is what allows us to struggle hard and long with tragedy or loss or misfortune or change and still manage to dig deep and find our second wind. It is a kind of toughness. Each life blow no longer shatters us like a hammer hitting brick; rather it makes us stronger. It tempers us, like a hammer hitting metal. Imagine the comfort in knowing, that by never giving up, by accepting the bad breaks and going on, you have lived life to the fullest and maybe will have lived it a little longer. Such peace of mind is often reward enough."

Mrs. Helen Bandyke, 1998

Mrs. Cynthia Mayberry

"Everyone stands back and watches as the ball drops from the blue sky and lands securely into my left-handed mitt. 'He's safe!' I hear one of my brothers shout from home plate."

There's a house on Hanlon Street in Westland, Michigan, where I grew up as the only girl in the midst of three brothers. My life was a happy one as I recall. I learned at an early age to play all sports left-handed even though I was born right-handed. There was no doubt this girl on the block was the only one who possessed a "left-handed" mitt for baseball. You see, my three brothers were all lefties and, because of that, I learned at an early age the spirit of survival. Our parents are still married today after almost 50 years of being together. Our parents loved us kids, raised us with a value system, believed in discipline, took us to church and believed in a hard day's work for an honest day's pay.

My father worked in a steel plant in Redford, Michigan, all of his working years. My mother went to work as a postal employee in Wayne, Michigan, when I was 12.

My brothers and I attended public schools in Westland, which at that time was known as Nankin Township. We were a family who spent a lot of time together. We played games, hosted baseball games in our acre backyard, climbed huge oak trees, and visited our grandparents at least once a year because they lived out of state. We were basically a closely knit family who cared about the needs of each other. I can never remember in my entire childhood seeing alcohol or tobacco products in our home. I can never remember hearing my parents having an unkind word for one another.

Many children grow up and take their "childhood scars" with them into adulthood, scars that they hide from others and even themselves. The scars I share with you are scars that came not from my childhood but later in life. When I reflect upon the scars of my life, I wonder at times if the reason mine are so visible is to remind me forever of where I received these scars and to teach me a lesson to never go there again. Each scar I will share with you has only made me a better, stronger, more alive individual. Each scar I bear has renewed my faith, rekindled my spirit and restored my love for a God who never makes mistakes.

In 1971, I finished high school and decided to pursue an education in elementary teaching. After my undergraduate studies were complete, I began teaching second grade at the age of 22. I instantly fell in love with teaching the first day I stood before children and began to challenge their minds to think and to always ask questions. There is nothing like teaching children to stretch themselves to levels they have never been to before. Watching a child learn how to put letters together to make sounds, and then to words, then to make sentences, and on to paragraphs, and finally to create stories was incredible. Knowing that I had chosen a career with the opportunity to mold the lives of young people is as rewarding today as it was then.

After three years of teaching, I met a man who had custody of his three young children. In 1979 this was almost unheard of and just the fact that he loved his children so much drew me instantly to him. We had a short courtship and in 1980 we were married, thus making me the instant mother of Johnathan who was 7, Jeremy who was 6 and Valerie who was 5. It as not an easy task to take on three small children then, nor would it be today. To walk into instant parenthood, one can only imagine the mistakes I made along the way. Mistakes that were never intentional, but nevertheless at the expense of all involved. I continued my teaching career as I searched to find my role as a parent literally overnight. There were a great deal of laughter and warm moments raising Johnathan, Jeremy and Valerie. I have learned to keep those memories alive deep within my heart and many times use them to soothe the scars that were created along the way.

During the course of raising our three older children, we discovered that Johnathan was "profoundly deaf" and required medical attention during his entire growing years, including several surgeries, hearing aids, and on and on and on.

We also discovered that Valerie in her teen years was diagnosed with scoliosis, which required an equal amount of medical attention, including back braces, doctor appointments, etc. Although Jeremy suffered from no medical misfortunes, he missed his biological mother tremendously, thus bringing many years of discontentment and hurt.

A few years into our marriage, God blessed us with two beautiful children of our own, Christopher and Kathryn (Katie). For the first time in my life as a parent, I knew the depth of a love relationship between parent and child. I fell more in love with Chris and Katie each day. Both of our children had high medical needs. They were children who required hundreds of doctor visits, hospital stays, transfusions and endless hours of care. Blending our own children into an already made family did not seem very hard at the time; however, the scars came later and still remain today.

In 1988 when I was 34 years old, raising five children, teaching school, and sailing through life 100 miles per hour, a storm came into my life that I was not prepared to deal with at all. It was a cold, blustery February afternoon as I drove to see a man by the name of Dr. Waldinger. The wind was whipping around the trees and as it blew, one could feel the sting of Michigan winter in the air. The sun was shining bright; however, for some reason the sun did not hold the same warm affection in my soul as it had in previous days of my youth.

My mind began to reflect on all my days I had spent in the sun. Could anything that had given me so much physical pleasure at one time now be the cause for such immediate danger and concern? How could my previous years of an affair with the sun be the reason for this dreaded doctor appointment today?

There is nothing in the entire world like the feeling of the hot sun baking down from the sky onto your bare skin. The sensation and warmth that the hot sun brings with it are incredible. As your bare skin anxiously awaits and welcomes the penetration of the sun's rays into its pores, one can sense the heat that radiates deep within your bones.

Again I questioned how a love affair with the sun could go bad. My mind began to wander back to my teen years when I would lie afloat a 99-cent air mattress on a lake all day and bake my fair skin until it was so golden brown that my tan line would last easily until the Christmas season. And how about those college days and early into my teaching career when I thought Spring Break was the highlight of each calendar year. I remembered one time in my early 20s when I was so sunburned during Easter break that when I awoke the morning after a day at the beach, I fell down because my skin was so blistered I could not even stand.

How my mind was quickly brought back to the day's events as the warm sunshine was replaced by blowing snow and howling winds. My mission was very clear in my mind that day as I drove to see Dr. Waldinger. My mission was to get my husband and everyone else off my back. It seemed as though everyone in my family had become a doctor without a license to practice. Everyone was so concerned about this small, insignificant mole that had appeared on my inner right leg near my knee. How could such a small dark mole have so many people in such great alarm?

The drive that day seemed like such a waste of time for not only me but also for this doctor I had never met. My two small children were staying late in day care so I could make this appointment. Our three older children were in different sporting events. Time was ticking away; the day was getting later and later. Dinner would not be on time because of this appointment, day care would cost more, and on and on my thoughts went.

As I look back to almost 11 years since I first met Dr. Waldinger, I would have never thought a patient could grow to love and respect a physician as I have this man. It was Dr. Waldinger's diligence intertwined with his compassion that set him aside from all the rest. There was something very special about Dr. Waldinger that provided me with an instant trust in him. I sensed in Dr. Waldinger that he knew his limits as an earthly physician and left the rest up to our Heavenly physician. He took one look at my leg and told me point blank in his professional opinion I had a malignant melanoma that needed immediate attention. He proceeded to do a biopsy in his office that day. He sent me on my way and told me he would call me as soon as he had heard something.

Less than one week went by and the phone call came. Indeed it was this same man I had only met one week earlier, and with his voice came that dreaded news. My biopsy had come back. It was certain I had a malignant melanoma. A wide margin removal was my only option at this point. Knowing very little about melanoma, but knowing enough to know that this type of cancer is a most aggressive killer, I decided not to argue with this doctor. The appointment was made at the University of Michigan in Ann Arbor, Michigan, and that was that.

Suddenly I felt as though my life were not mine to make decisions for any longer. I hung up the phone that day with a mind that was racing to find the answers to all the questions I had. My thoughts were incredible. How could someone like myself who had never smoked or had never drunk, someone who had gone to church all her life, be dealt such a harsh diagnosis like cancer? I had five children yet to raise. My baby was only two and was just coming out of her own major medical problems. I was in the prime of my life and way too busy to stop and deal with all that was happening to me.

Then I began to feel a deep loss, as though something had been taken away from me before I was ready to let go, or without my permission. I began to feel guilty and wonder if some sin in my life prior to this disease is what gave me this cancer. Perhaps the doctor was wrong. Perhaps I did not have cancer. Maybe they had me mixed up with some other female. The questions kept coming, never stopping, never giving me the chance to collect my thoughts or even develop a plan of action. I went from anger to denial to depression. Within a week I was at the University of Michigan in Ann Arbor being prepped for surgery.

I can remember asking God to allow me enough days to see my children grow up. Now I ask God to allow me enough days to see my grandchildren grow up. The asking of God never stops, for there is no good time to say goodbye to the people you love.

So another scar was placed on my body. This one was very visible and a constant reminder of my carefree days in the sun. I found in order for me to stay out of the sun I had to ask God to take my love and passion away that I had once had with the sun. I began to ask God to help me fall more in love with His Son rather than the sun I had so foolishly worshipped in past years.

Each day began to look different for me. I wanted to live my life to the fullest because the more I read about melanoma the more I began to realize how blessed I was that God had for some reason spared my life. There was an overwhelming desire to kill the cancer instead of allowing the cancer to kill me.

My children and the little things they did became much more precious to my life. I began to take the extra time needed to listen and play and care and nurture. I held my children in my lap for hours at a time. I never minded and still don't when my children wake me in the wee hours of the night for comfort. I hug my children every day and tell them how much I love them and what they mean to me. Fixing special meals is not a burden to me but instead a delight. Some say I have spoiled my children over the years. I choose to say I have loved them as much as I can, realizing just how precious each day I have with them is.

My teaching career took on a more powerful attitude because I wasn't so sure at this time just what was happening to my life. My desire to continue my education became paramount. I enrolled at Eastern Michigan University as a graduate student in the summer of 1991 and 13 months later I had taken 34 graduate credits and received a Master's Degree in Educational Leadership. Motivated and driven I was for sure. The summer of 1992 I took Christopher and Katie by myself on a 31-day, 7,500-mile road trip to the Grand Canyon and back. The power I felt was incredible. Every moment of every day had to be explored. People still accuse me of "packing in" way too many things in a 24-hour period. Every minute of every day must be a celebration of life.

However, in my quest to do the things I wanted to do, my relationship with my husband began to dissolve. By the middle of 1994, my marriage had ended and with it came more scars. The real, visible kind. The kind nobody can hide. My life had not only lost the sunshine I once loved, but it had also lost the sunlight of my life.

For three years I searched for some sunshine in my life. There were times when I wanted nothing more than to fly to a warm climate, put on a bathing suit, take off my hat and sunglasses, wear no sun block and just allow the sun to take my life from me.

But those two precious children God spared my life to see raised are what kept me going. Their smiles would remind me each day that life is worth living. They would remind me each morning that I did have a reason to keep on going, in spite of the scars that life had brought my way.

I began to find sunshine within my inner soul for the first time in a long time. I began to realize that scars are not so bad after all. For you see, if a person can learn from the scars of life, hopefully they will never have the same scars twice.

I continued to look at my scars in a different light and after many hours, days, weeks and even years, I finally allowed my scars to teach me lessons that I intend to keep deep within my heart for the rest of my living days. If it means that I deliberately look at my scars each day to remind me never to revisit places again that created the scars to begin with, then that is what I'll do.

Scars have a remarkable way of healing deep wounds. In October of 1997, my husband, Gary, and I were remarried.

What a spiritual healing for both of us! We both had learned some valuable lessons from the scars of life. I had learned that God had spared my life from a physical disease called cancer, not to have me die a spiritual death. God had been so gracious, allowing me more days on this earth and I was going through life acting as though it was my right. Life is such a precious gift, and each day we wake up and see the sunshine we should say, "Thank You, God."

When I needed a physical healing, it was the spiritual healing that came to me and granted me more days, weeks, months, even years to live. It was the spiritual healing that came to me and gave me a peace to accept what I could not ever change. It was the spiritual healing that allowed me to accept God's perfect plan for my life in having the experience of cancer. For had I not had this experience, I am certain that my heart would have never been tender enough to start over with my husband, the father of our children.

Cancer is not a bad thing. Only if you let it become one. Yes, it takes lives without the permission of the ones it invades. Yes, it shortens years and events for people and the ones they love. But cancer is also something that you must embrace.

If you don't embrace the pain, you will never allow yourself to grow from the pain or the scars that cancer leaves. Cancer shows people how urgent each day is. It teaches people that life is too short to be angry and hateful toward their brothers and sisters. It teaches one to treat each new day with a level of respect for the one who gave you breath.

My mind wanders back to my childhood days and to our baseball field on Hanlon Street in Westland, Michigan. One of my brothers slams the ball right to me. I reach out my left-handed mitt to catch the fly ball, knowing it doesn't matter whether I am right- or left-handed. What matters is that I have the courage to reach out my mitt and catch the ball. I call it. "It's mine. It's mine." Everyone stands back and watches as the ball drops from the blue sky and lands securely into my left-handed mitt. "He's safe!" I hear one of my brothers shout from home plate.

Thirty-five years later does it matter if the person on third was out or safe? What matters is we stayed in the game and kept playing. It's kind of like life, don't you think?

Cancer and the scars it leaves will change your life forever if you keep your heart tender to the sunshine. Bask in the sunlight He has to offer you. Allow His rays to soak deep into your soul. Feel the warmth that only He can provide. Hold strong to the promises that He will never leave you or forsake you. Believe in miracles and when you have experienced one, be ready to share it with someone else who needs to hear your story. Pray for courage to accept the things you cannot change. Stay in the game even if your mitt doesn't fit.

And you and the people who love you the most will never be the same. . .ever again.

Commentary:

> "To be what we are, and to become what we are
> capable of becoming is the only end of life."
> – Spinoza

Mrs. Cynthia Mayberry, age 2, and her dad, Christmas Eve on Hanlon Street, Westland, Michigan, 1955

Mrs. Teresa Dickie

"I know it has made me appreciate even more the beauty of a wondrous sunrise or sunset, the joy of spring and the value of friendships old and new."

To anyone who has heard these words, "I'm afraid it is cancer," you know how your stomach hits the floor, your heart pounds as though it were coming out of your chest, and your whole life flies before your eyes.

It was my beloved father's 79th birthday and he and my mother had come to visit me in the hospital after my "successful" thyroid surgery in 1993. There was a stillness in that curtained area that a knife could cut. I could see how difficult it was for the surgeon to continue to tell me that further surgery would be necessary. I could tell my dad was shrinking inside and wondering why it wasn't him instead of me. I could feel he was visibly shaken, and I had the usual first selfish thought, "Why me?" My mind raced that perhaps I would never see my youngest graduate from high school, or my eldest, who had just graduated the previous week, get married. Why only last night when Ron had visited, although I was still nauseous from the anesthesia, we had begun to believe we were home safe and sound.

My journey to this point had begun several months earlier when my doctor had discovered a lump in my neck and suggested I have it examined further. It was the thyroid gland that was cancerous. I found myself on a familiar journey through corridors, white-painted and austere, to another pristine, cool and, apart from the swish of machinery, quiet operating room. This time I was very hesitant about what lay ahead of me. I was fighting the "Big C." So now I am still traveling, although there have been many periods of doubt on my part.

In order to make sure that all the cancerous cells had been removed, I had to undergo radiation called an ablation. This is where you are in isolation for up to three days after you had taken a "lethal cocktail" of radioactive material. It was during this time that I was able to really think about my life, the people in it, what was I going to do about this demon I was trying to exorcise from my body, and how I would deal with life in the future.

The preparations that go on before you are left in the room on your own leave little to the imagination of how strong a medicine this radiation is: Everything you are likely to touch is covered in plastic or paper, the route from the bed to the bathroom is mapped out like stepping stones and you do begin to feel that you are indeed a leper who must be kept at arm's length. Your vital signs are taken and then you are asked to take this cup out of a lead container and, with the straw provided, drink it down in one smooth swallow. It is tasteless and odorless, but obviously it is very powerful, because immediately the technician leaves the room and says she will return in the morning.

Your meals are slid around the corner of the door, your vital signs are checked at arm's length and by the end of the first day, your room looks like a motel room on a rainy day when no one can go out, and the trash keeps building up!

My sanity was saved because the room had a window and I knew that there was a world outside. I did have a telephone and a television but had no contact with the human touch, although the nurses would buzz me periodically to make sure I was all right. It was during this time when the seconds ticked by on the clock ever so slowly that I imagined what the hostages during the Iran crisis must have felt like. Here I was in isolation like they had been kept, although the subtle difference was that I was surrounded with kind human beings and knew that my time

Ron and Teresa Dickie with family, 1998

in solitary would end soon. It was here that I really came to terms with my condition. I had always been a religious person, although for years now I had not attended church on a regular basis, but had and still have a tremendous faith in God. That was one reason why I felt "let-down" by Him when I had received the news that I had been diagnosed with cancer. However, when I made a litany of all the requests I had made of Him, and all the positive answers I had received from Him, I realized that really I was still on the plus side.

Since that time in 1993, I have had several brushes with hospitals, surgeries, tests, etc., and so far I am still ahead of the game. I do have to take medication now every day for the rest of my life because I have no thyroid at all. It is amazing what that little gland governs. Whenever I have to undergo a body scan every couple of years, I have to come off the medication for six weeks and, by the time I enter the third week, my energy level is such that to make a cup of tea feels like you have won an Olympic gold medal! Your weight skyrockets, as does your cholesterol level, you cry for no reason, your skin looks and feels like a crocodile, headaches pop up out of nowhere and many other annoying things. However, once you are back on the medication, within a few days these annoyances pass. One of the things that I do thank God for is my family, because they are very helpful during these "down-times."

Another wonderful example I had to follow was my dear friend, Sarah, who unfortunately lost her battle with cancer a couple of years ago. She would never give up. Whenever her cancer appeared in another part of her body, she would pick up her battle cry of "Oh, well, here we go again, Sarah" and she would try every pill and potion that may have an effect on the disease that was eating her up.

When you have stared in the face the possible ending of your life, you realize that what you have is worth fighting for. Also you appreciate life after selfishly thinking at first that life is against you. There are people who are worse off than you for many reasons, and the "Why me?" syndrome becomes the "Why NOT me?" I am not going to say there have not been times that I have felt very sorry for myself, have felt discarded by God, and thoughts of suicide become a very warm comforting feeling until the fighter inside of you revs up and you feel the blood flow through your veins as you prepare for the next round.

I hope that my experience with modern society's number one fear has made me more understanding. I know it has made me appreciate even more the beauty of a wondrous sunrise or sunset, the joy of spring and the value of friendships old and new. I have always had total faith in those who have treated me and even when doubts have been raised which have necessitated another test, you keep on hoping that at some point it is going to have a positive outcome. There have been many nights, which have been long and scary awaiting results, and when the light of dawn comes, the world seems to have a softer edge to it and hope springs eternal. I realize now how important the little things in life have become. I try, although not always successfully, to give a little more time to those around me who are lonely and without support. I tell my children to try if possible never to leave friends or family in an angry mood because you never know what is going to happen to you or them and perhaps you may never get another chance to say goodbye or that you love them.

My dear father, who passed away over four years ago, together with my mother, who is still with me, raised me to honor them and help others as much as we can. Since my dealings with cancer, I have come to realize how true these ideals are.

Commentary:

"True wisdom lies in gathering the precious things out of each day as it goes by."

– E.S. Bouton

Mrs. Jan Smith

"Life presents many challenges, but it also equips us to meet them."

Having been a patient of Dr. Ulrich's beginning in the 1960s and then later one of Dr. Waldinger's patients and employees, I was delighted to be asked to contribute a philosophy statement to this book. I remember that as a teenager I was touched by Dr. Ulrich's kindness, his sincere question at the start of each office visit of "How are you, angel?" and, of course, the excellent medical care he provided. Certainly, Dr. Waldinger is the perfect successor to Dr. Ulrich because he carries the same high standards of excellence and compassion in treating his patients. Both of these physicians, like so many of the people I have had the pleasure of encountering in life, have undoubtedly positively affected the lives of more individuals than they would imagine.

Thinking about this philosophy statement has only emphasized for me my long-held belief that how we choose to interact with the people we live and work with, meet on a daily basis, or maybe meet just once in a lifetime, is fundamental to how we experience life. Right now with family activities and commitments being what they are, I find I do not always take much time to write down my thoughts about life. As my mother, who is in her late 80s, points out, one day later on in life there may well be too much free time again, and I will cherish the memories of these busy times, wishing I had some of those same things to fill my days again.

I consider it a true blessing to have had a close, supportive family. My parents have always demonstrated their love, concern and generosity to their three daughters and their families. Beginning as a child, in fact, I was naively puzzled when I began to notice that not all siblings were as fortunate as we sisters were to share a closeness that transcended a 12-year age difference from youngest to oldest and many geographical separations over the years. Often my sisters and I joke that we share a mental, almost telepathic bond. Why did I feel the urge years ago to interrupt a vacation in Berchtesgaden, Germany, to return to my home in Mainz to find the telegram announcing my nephew's birth? Something drew me home, and perhaps it was nothing more than coincidence. However, I often feel drawn to contact my sisters and mother without realizing what it is that's calling us together only to discover that they have had a similar feeling.

This close family bond, also enjoyed with my father when he was alive, has helped me learn about love, spirituality, compassion, loyalty, humor, sadness, hard work and a host of other aspects of life and the human condition. My family has always been there as I've dealt with whatever life has brought me and given me an awareness of how to savor that which is good in people and learn from those around us. Life's lessons come in the most unexpected places and from the most unexpected events—desired or undesired. There is always something to learn from what life presents and growth comes from learning to deal with whatever comes your way without losing faith.

At times of a parent's or young nephew's death, the prolonged pain and illness of a dear one, depression suffered by a loved one, miscarriages, separations, unkindness, anger and despair, the challenge is always to remain steady, strong and focused on constants, such as religious beliefs. My father always reminded me "this too shall pass." These are all parts of life.

The examples of behavior modeled in my parents' love, respect for each other, strength of character and integrity are still inspirational to me. Throughout his over 50 years in banking, starting ironically enough, at the time of the Great Depression, my father always showed a keen interest in people and his dealings with them were permeated with kindness and respect. I feel they sensed his genuine interest in them and their concerns and responded positively to that.

As a wife and parent myself, I hope I am sharing with my husband and daughters the essence of what I feel I was fortunate to learn at home. Both my husband, David, and I realize and appreciate what an awesome responsibility it is to be a parent. I may not have thought much at the time about hearing at home "We love you," "You're doing great," and "Keep up the good work," "Give it your best," "You can do it," and "The Lord never gives you any challenge you can't handle." Now I realize how much encouragement and faith can do.

It couldn't have been easy for my parents to watch me go to Germany to study and work when I wasn't yet 21. Their support allowed me the opportunity to pursue a field of study I love and let me experience what it's like to make your way in another culture using a foreign language. That experience definitely shapes my thinking still and provides me coping skills to this day. Those skills certainly were of help as my husband and I relocated numerous times, far from family, during his career as an Army officer. Whenever we went to a new location, we always made a home and were blessed to connect with many wonderful people. We did have too many goodbyes to say, but also learned to realize and enjoy what each new location presented us. Kindness received often couldn't be returned directly to the givers because they had moved on, but we learned to be grateful and pass on the good deed to someone else, even if in another place and time.

Life presents many challenges, but it also equips us to meet them. The joy in doing so comes from our faith, our attitude, our initiative and our responses to people and things around us. My final thought is that life is a precious gift to be appreciated and used as it was intended. It is worth one's best efforts—we never know where some small, seemingly inconsequential deed or happening can lead. That's the challenge and fun of seeing where the journey leads.

As a parting thought, I'm including a portion of one of my favorite closings from our worship services at church:

"Go out into the world in peace;
have courage;
hold on to what is good;
return no one evil for evil;
strengthen the fainthearted;
support the weak, help the suffering;
honor all people;
love and serve the Lord,
rejoicing in the power of the Holy Spirit."

Mrs. Smith (center) and her sisters, Gretchen and Kathryn, 1949

Commentary:

During my first year of practice, Dr. Ulrich encouraged me to join the Dearborn Rotary Club. I had lived in Ann Arbor for the past 14 years and did not know anyone in Dearborn. The club met each Thursday at lunchtime. I had lunch with many wonderful people and was fortunate to develop new friends. One of them was Mr. Ralph Wagner, Jan's father.

I concur with Jan that her father showed, "a keen interest in people and his dealings were permeated with kindness and respect." Mr. Wagner passed away in July of 1990 and will be remembered always.

Jan, I am so fortunate to know you and your family throughout the years. I am even more fortunate to have you as a new member of my staff. Your father's wisdom and philosophy of life continue with you.

———————— ❖ ————————

Dr. Donald Mys

*". . .he proceeded to put a penny into each of my pockets
and patches on my bib overalls."*

Two characteristics come to my mind immediately when I ponder my philosophy of life. The first is fairness and the second, perseverance.

My early childhood was spent in a farming community situated in the middle of Michigan where I attended a one-room schoolhouse from kindergarten through eighth grade. I walked the one mile to Highland #1 School each day as did my three older brothers and two older sisters. There were a total of three students in my class when I graduated!

While I was growing up, I was expected to do many tasks. I had first-hand experience hauling hay, driving tractors, assembling farm machinery, and harvesting potatoes, pickles and green beans. Also, since my father owned the Ina General Store and an International Harvester farm-equipment dealership, I learned how to stock shelves with groceries and hardware, pump gasoline, and sell customers groceries and parts for their farm equipment. I quickly learned the rewards of working hard, serving the public fairly and the value of earning my own money.

One memory that stays with me to this day was when my Uncle Pete from Iowa visited our family. He was considered to be our "'rich uncle" as he took each of us for a ride in his new

Dr. Donald Mys in his bib overalls, 1947

Model "A" Ford. At the end of his visit he gave each one of my brothers and sisters a dollar bill. I was only 5 or 6 years old at the time, and he proceeded to put a penny into each of my pockets and patches on my bib overalls. All I received was 13 cents! I didn't think it was fair that I didn't get a dollar like all of the others. Being fair was a lesson that I never forgot and this concept has remained with me to this day.

After graduating from grade school, high school and college, I began teaching high school mathematics at Lowrey School in Dearborn. I vividly recall the very first day of my teaching career. An unforgettable situation occurred in my first hour Algebra class. I knew that I would have to make special arrangements in presenting my Algebra lessons on the blackboard because I was assigned a student with a hearing impairment. This meant that whenever I was writing the math problems on the blackboard, I would have to turn toward the class and speak directly to this student because he would need to read my lips in order to comprehend. You can then imagine my dilemma when in walked another "challenged" student with a visual impairment. She was blind and was unable to see the blackboard. My job then was to explain in detail every step of each math problem that I was writing on the blackboard so that the blind student could visualize it. I also had to make sure to turn toward the hearing impaired student at the same time. That semester sharpened my teaching strategies a great deal and was an unforgettable experience. But I persevered and made sure that I was fair to both of my two special students and the entire class.

I have enjoyed my involvement in serving the community and was active in leadership roles at Cherry Hill Presbyterian Church and with the Dearborn Rotary Club. At church I served as a Ruling Elder for two sessions, Chairman of the Christian Education Department, Chairman of the Youth Minister Selection Committee, and as Stewardship Chairman when we raised nearly one-third of a million dollars. For 10 years I had perfect attendance at the Dearborn Rotary Club, served as a member of the Rotary Foundation Board, was Youth Chairman and Blood Drive Chairman. In 1987, I was named a Paul Harris

Fellow by Rotary Foundation of Rotary International, to which I was very proud to be of service.

Professionally, I served as President and Treasurer of the Dearborn Schools Administrative Association and received the DSAA "Administrator of the Year" award in 1992. I had the privilege of making a number of research presentations to colleagues within the Dearborn Public Schools, to educators at the Michigan Educational Research Association and at the National School Board Association Institute for the Transfer of Technology to Education at Dallas, Texas.

My career in education included teaching at the high school, junior high school and university levels. My administrative experience included being the Coordinator of the Testing, Research and Evaluation Office for over 20 years and my years as an assistant principal at Fordson High School. The issue of fairness to students also comes to mind when I was responsible for the discipline of some 500 ninth grade students. I always made sure that I gave each young adult the chance to state his or her side before a decision was made when administering the Student Code of Conduct.

Being fair in what I do with my family or other people has been an important goal in my life. A person must be fair in order to be able to deal effectively with others. In my past and present leadership roles I have always tried to include fairness. All components of leadership lead to fairness. Fairness does not seem to be prominent in life today and too many unfair things are happening to good people. We must all understand and practice fairness in life. I'm confident we will all be better human beings as a result.

When I was an assistant principal at Fordson High School, I was dealt a problem which nearly shattered my life. I suffered a heart attack which left me with one-third of my heart permanently damaged. My recovery of health has been slow but with promising progress. We have persevered with God's help.

Commentary:

I initially met Dr. Donald Mys at the Rotary Club in Dearborn in 1985. He then became a patient and valued friend. All effective leadership must be based on fairness and ethical values. Although leadership encompasses many attributes, without fairness leadership is vacuous. The Rotary motto is a guide for all human interaction as well as the basis for leadership. It states SERVICE ABOVE SELF®.

The Rotary 4-Way Test of things we think, say or do is a foundation for leadership. It is as follows:

1. Is it the TRUTH?
2. Is it FAIR to all concerned?
3. Will it build GOODWILL and BETTER FRIENDSHIPS?
4. Will it be BENEFICIAL to all concerned?

Bill Bradley in his book *Values of the Game* eloquently writes about leadership:

"Leadership means getting people to think, believe, see, and do what they might not have without you. It means possessing the vision to set the right goal and the decisiveness to pursue it single-mindedly. It means being aware of the fears and anxieties felt by those you lead even as you urge them to overcome those fears. It can appear in a speech before hundreds of people or in a dialogue with one other person—or simply by example. . . .The great leaders in basketball have never been afraid of change and they have led from the strength of their own convictions. And, above all, they have brought out the best in the people they lead."

Faith, Service, Compassion, Acceptance

Faith, service, compassion for others and acceptance are the focal points of the next philosophy of life statements. As I look back, the death of Dr. Ulrich created a great void in my life. My patients and their wisdom have helped fill that void.

Dr. Robert Young wrote in his philosophy of life statement, "Thanks much, and look forward. Look back only to learn." I look back each day, remembering the wisdom and benevolence of Dr. Ulrich. I look forward each day, grateful for the new philosophies my patients offer and subsequent connections.

Love and faithfulness meet together;
righteousness and peace kiss each other.

– Psalm 85:10

Mrs. Helen Holody

"For what does it profit a man. . . ."

Looking back on my life from this vantage of my 57th year reveals how loving was that counsel provided by our Lord when he wisely advised, "For what does it profit a man if he gain the whole world and suffer the loss of his soul." In retrospect, I see how this admonition has directly influenced how I live and the decisions I make. Life is a journey, and how I live this life will determine what kind of an afterlife I will have.

Many other influences have also contributed to my philosophy of life. My life has been blessed by Providence with wonderful parents, a loving and devoted husband and good, faithful children. First, it was my parents who gave me their philosophy of life through their love, discipline, sacrifices and example. I was the second oldest in a family of seven children. My parents always demonstrated much love for us which included the right amount of discipline. Their sacrifices were numerous, one of the biggest of which was putting all of us through parochial school, which had a major impact on my life. Most important of all was their example. They not only taught us how to live but also showed us. They were extremely devoted to one another, always putting their Catholic faith and God first in their lives. Their marriage was a mirror of the

Trinity—my father, my mother and God. They were happy, not because there were no trials, but because they had the hope that faith in God and His promised afterlife (heaven) ensures.

We had our share of tragedies. My youngest sister, Anita, was born with cerebral palsy along with a spastic condition, which left her like a baby all her life. She could not sit unassisted, let alone walk and talk and use her hands. My parents believed that God gave them this special soul to care for until He called her home. And so they cared for her (especially my mother) in their home until my mother became ill with cancer and Anita was put in a nursing home nearby. Every day, my mother went to the nursing home to feed my sister lunch and dinner but, more than that, to give her love and affection. When my mother died, my father took over this role, caring for Anita until her death at the age of 33.

I remember when I was in college someone had advised my parents that they should put my sister in a nursing home because her presence in our home might ruin their children's chances of finding a husband or wife. I told my mother, "I wouldn't have wanted to marry the kind of man who wouldn't want to marry me because of Anita."

Another tragedy that occurred at the beginning of my senior year in high school was the death of my brother, who was two years younger than I. He was accidentally shot in the back of the head while hunting with some acquaintances from school. The young man who shot him was devastated. He apologized to my parents and asked their forgiveness. My parents and all of us forgave him, but it was extremely difficult. Without God and our Catholic faith and the hope that it gave us, we could not have forgiven the young man nor made it through those difficult days after my brother's death. The impact of my brother's death on my life was far-reaching. I had heard it said over and over that I should live my life as if I would die tomorrow because I do not know when God will call me home. But somehow I didn't think it would ever happen to me. I pictured myself living to a ripe old age. Then suddenly my brother, who was very close to me, died at 15 years of age. This was the cause of much reflection on my own life. I suddenly realized that the Lord could call me home at an early age and that I must be ready to meet Him.

At the recent canonization of Edith Stein, Pope John Paul II noted that suffering pointed the way to the truth of the cross when he said, "Don't accept anything as truth if it is without love. And don't accept anything as love if it is without truth! One without the other is a harmful lie. . . . Many of our contemporaries would want the cross made silent! The true message of pain is a lesson of love. Love makes pain bear fruit and pain deepens love."

From my vantage now and his comments, I could see a deeper lesson about evil in these two events. The suffering by my sister, Anita, and the devotion with which first my mother and then my father cared for her showed how pain is compelling testimony of love to those, such as me, who are blessed to witness it in truth. Selfless love of life is victor over lifeless love of the self. In the death of my brother, one can see an especially unspeakable evil, the wonton and impersonal universe of the nihilist, where random acts show that if there is a God, He is reckless and uncaring, and therefore not to be relied upon. Here a simple and direct forgiveness of an inestimable grievance transforms an otherwise horrid universe into a poignant reminder of another great admonition of our Lord, "to be in the world, but not of the world." When I was in high school, a nun in one of my religion classes once said, "When you look for a husband or wife, you should choose someone who will help you get to heaven." And my grandmother told me that you do not reach heaven or hell alone; you always bring somebody with you. With this in mind, I married my loving and devoted husband of 35 years. Paul has been the greatest influence in my life. Certainly, he has been one of God's greatest gifts to me. Possessing a keen mind and a quick wit, he has shown much wisdom throughout his life. My husband has been a source of great strength for me because he is a man of principle who has the courage of his convictions. He is not afraid to say no when everyone else is saying yes.

We have grown in our faith together, often struggling to make sense of all the changes occurring in the Catholic Church after Vatican II. Our biggest struggle has been in raising our three sons with traditional values when the world surrounding us has been just the opposite. When our boys were ready for school, we sent them to a newly founded parent-run Catholic school. This was not an easy choice because many hours were spent volunteering on various committees for fund raising, teacher selection, etc. and I served on its board for eight years, four years as president. However, long-lasting friendships were formed with other parents sending their children to this special school. Their influence provided us with the strength and the courage necessary to make hard decisions in our faith and in the raising of our children. It seems our efforts have been rewarded because our sons, who are now in their late 20s and early 30s, share our traditional values and are strong in their faith.

As my husband and I approach our 60s and our sons are getting married, we look forward to grandchildren, retirement and whatever else Providence has for us and–should we be so presumptuous–to what St. Augustine spoke of when he said, "Our hearts shall not rest until they rest in Thee."

Mrs. Helen Holody and family, Salzburg, Austria, August 1988

Mr. Walter Orr

"Many years later after I had grown up, married and moved away, the lesson became clear."

I was born in a small farm town in Tennessee. I was the third of five children and the only son of Myrtle and Leonard Orr. I guess my life was much like other children's in our area, one that of hard work, few material things, and lots of unspoken love. Unspoken, because both my parents were deaf mutes. My mother and two of her sisters were born deaf, and my father always said his deafness was caused by a mule kick to the head when he was a 4-year-old child.

One of my duties as I grew up was to accompany my father to the general store. He would sign to me and in turn I would tell the storekeeper what my father wanted. If the clerk needed to tell my father something, I would listen and then sign back to my dad. As we would be going through this procedure, people would gather around and stare at us. I would become so embarrassed and angry that I wanted to shout, "What are you looking at, what's wrong with you?" If my dad would just write it down, I wouldn't have to go through this! But he didn't; he depended on me to be his ears and his mouth. Maybe he was embarrassed or afraid he wouldn't know what was being said to him and he needed me, his only son, to be there. Whatever the reason, I didn't like it, but nonetheless it was a task I undertook.

Many years later after I had grown up, married and moved away, the lesson became clear. When I would see someone with a physical or mental handicap, I felt empathy. I didn't want to stare. I would nod my head in recognition to let them know that they had worth, that they were someone of value. The lesson I had learned in the old country store was one of compassion. A lesson learned from a silent, gentle father.

Walter and Violet Orr, newly married, and his parents, 1943

Dr. Margaret Warrick

"I truly wanted to reach out to anyone in the audience who was dealing with something painful or sad and have their sense of spirit, if even for a moment, vicariously be in tandem with mine."

Of all of his patients, I, perhaps, have had the longest association with Dr. Waldinger. I began seeing Dr. Waldinger while he was a resident in training at the University of Michigan, and I was a graduate student, using the resources of the student health center. Dr. Waldinger treats my keloids (scar tissue that continues to form after trauma to the skin). The scars Dr. Waldinger has treated over the past 18 years are somewhat a road map for the events that have shaped my life and reinforced my values and philosophies. These include unselfishness, empathy toward others, finding the positive in people and in difficult situations, and overall always maintaining a sense of humor. Though many people and experiences have reinforced and guided these values and philosophies, I primarily credit my father for teaching unselfishness and humility, my mother for imparting the value of always looking for the positive, a nurse for giving me hope, and my friends for reinforcing the joy and power of humor.

I grew up in the 1950s in a very secure and loving home. As the middle child, I had parents who never let me feel sorry for myself even though I had an unsightly scar on my left arm. The early lesson in finding good in bad involved this scar. My parents pointed out that I was lucky because with my scar I could easily tell my left from my right. When I was about 8 years old, I was accompanying my dad on his Saturday errands (something I always loved to do) when we became lost and were suddenly driving through a very economically depressed neighborhood. We came upon three kids trying to use an old bike tire as a hula-hoop. My dad suddenly stopped the car and opened the trunk where my sister's, my brother's and my hula-hoops had been placed in preparation for a picnic later that day. He gave those poor children the hula-hoops. I watched this action somewhat in dismay. When my dad returned to the car, I looked at him with a combination of anger and pride. After all, he had just given away my hula-hoop! I started to say something, but then he faced me, ready to explain his actions. Suddenly I knew he didn't have to and he then also knew he didn't have to. It was my first true lesson in unselfish giving.

While visiting my then fiancé in San Diego in 1985, I was involved in a near fatal car accident. I won't go into all the details. Suffice it to say, I gave Dr. Waldinger a whole new set of scars to work on! Being on a respirator is probably the most horrible experience one can have, next to thinking that death is imminent. Again, I touch on the theme of unselfishness and the value of someone reaching out to help another. About a day or two after I was taken off the respirator and upgraded to intensive care, I became incredibly frightened about death. It was late at night when Mary, an African-American nurse with a beautiful round face, came into my room. I had never seen this nurse before. She came to my bedside and asked if something was wrong and why I wasn't asleep. I told her, with tears running down my cheeks, that I was afraid that if I closed my eyes I'd never wake up again. She took my hand and said that she would hold on to it, stay by my bed, and make sure I didn't die. She was so sweet and so comforting, her compassion and empathy so profound, that I trusted her and soon drifted off to sleep. I never saw Mary again. I greatly wish that I could because, more than the wonderful paramedics, surgeons and physicians who treated me through this trauma, I credit Mary for giving me hope and saving my life.

Surviving a traumatic car accident seems enough for one person, but in 1990, I heard those three dreaded words "You have cancer." And, unfortunately, I heard those words two more times–in 1991 and 1994. Like one out of eight women, I have experienced breast cancer. My dealings with breast cancer have taught me persistence, humility and the constant reminder that life is a precious gift and that one should never take anything or anyone for granted. And, once again, I gave Dr. Waldinger new scars to work on.

It may seem odd to say this, but I think having had to deal with cancer has not been a curse, but a gift. I have this special secret. Unlike so many people who just go through life and sort of go through the motions, I know that one must truly live life. I was laughing with my best friend one weekend when visiting her in Cleveland. After a late Friday night and a very full Saturday day and evening ahead, I was up at 5:30 in the morning getting ready to make a 6 a.m. tee time with her husband. Lynn called out from their bedroom and said, "Marg, I can't believe you are doing this!" I poked my head in and, with a big smile, said, "Well, see this is the curse of having had cancer. I feel compelled to live each day to the fullest!"

Besides teaching one to live life to the fullest, cancer also teaches you to keep the proper perspective on situations and challenges. I often think of a close friend who was diagnosed with breast cancer about a year before I was. Linda was not as lucky as I am. Many times when there is something I don't want to do or face, I think, "I bet Linda would rather be in my position than in her position." Unfortunately, Linda has passed away.

I also look to my mother, a recent widow, who has a severe hearing loss and in the last year was diagnosed with macular degeneration. At 83, she has incredible fortitude, energy and spirit. She never feels sorry for herself; on the contrary, she continually remarks about how lucky she is to have great children and friends and her health.

Humor has played a major role in my life and I credit my parents, who both had great wits, and my plethora of friends who love to laugh. In even the most trying cases, one can find a humorous side although this sometimes happens after the fact. Humor often is tragedy plus time. My closest friends never let me lose my sense of humor during my whole recuperative period after my car accident and during the three times I battled breast cancer.

Music and singing are also major forces in my life. I have always felt quite blessed that I could sing. Singing not only gives me a myriad of opportunities, but also provides me with a constant source of joy. It is hard to articulate the inner thrill I feel when performing great choral masterpieces such as Handel's "Messiah." When I was fairly certain that I was not going to die after my car accident, my fears turned to thoughts that I would never sing again. With a collapsed lung and most ribs broken, I had great difficulty breathing. I remember so clearly lying in that hospital bed trying to come to grips with the thought that I would never sing the "Hallelujah Chorus" again. As the weeks and months slowly passed, the driving force for me in my recuperation became completing all the painful healing therapy not only to be able to stand up straight and walk, but also to be able to sing. After the June accident, I have never stood so proudly and with such humble gratitude to God as I did that following December when I stood on stage at Hill Auditorium in Ann Arbor and sang the "Hallelujah Chorus" with all my heart.

Of course, along with all my concern about singing, I worried about performing. In recent years I had become quite involved in Gilbert and Sullivan productions. To think that I would no longer be able to dance, move around on a stage, and experience the great joy of entertaining an audience were equally devastating. It was more than a year before I had finally regained enough strength and mobility to be back on stage, performing in a lively Gilbert and Sullivan production.

I refused to let breast cancer interfere with performing even though the director had to modify some of my movements. In the first production I appeared in after my first mastectomy, I was determined to succeed. Maybe because of pain, embarrassment and fatigue, it is tempting to turn away from life, but

because life is so pre-
cious, one has to turn
into life, to embrace it. I
remember returning to
the stage after having
recovered from my first
mastectomy. I somehow
wanted to be able to
transmit to the audience
a message that would
have gone something
like this: "Look at me. I
am singing and dancing
and making you laugh,
and guess what? I've

Dr. Margaret Warrick (left) with best friend Lynn, 1995

had cancer, and I'm beating it, and so can you! You can beat any obstacle, if you have hope and joy in your heart. I truly wanted to reach out to anyone in the audience who was dealing with something painful or sad and have their sense of spirit, if even for a moment, vicariously be in tandem with mine."

It was my encounters with cancer, and my realization that I was given a second chance the night that Mary held my hand, which prompted me to change my career course. These experiences gave me the necessary lenses to see clearly that one's life's work should be work that has human value. The measure of success in a career is not the size of a paycheck, but the opportunity to make a positive difference in people's lives. Recently, I left a prestigious, but highly stressful, position to take a position in which I have the opportunity to impact children's lives. I'd like to think that I will have done my job well if I can impart to these children the critical values which have guided me in life and which I have touched on in the above biographical sketch. They are unselfish giving, finding the good in all situations and people, showing compassion and empathy toward others, keeping a positive outlook and attitude, and realizing the power of humor.

❖

Mrs. Georgia Joseph

يا عيني, تعي خذيني.

"Ya 'ainaya, Ta'ee Khu-thee-nee."
"My eyes, come and take me."

My birthplace was Bay City, Michigan. I am of Greek and Lebanese descent and the second oldest of five girls. We were raised with love by very strict parents. Religion was very important and I feel that is the reason I have such strong religious beliefs today. It was necessary for me to leave school in the ninth grade to work in my father's restaurant. I also did ironing for people and helped to care for my grandparents who spoke no English. This enabled me to speak fluent Lebanese.

My grandfather and two of his sons were blind. Their blindness was due to a hereditary eye disease. It is interesting to note that my mother was blind for approximately six months. She, however, sought treatment at the University of Michigan Medical Center and her sight was restored.

Our family resided with my blind grandfather. He had partial vision at one time, but because he refused to go for diagnosis and appropriate medical care, he eventually lost all of his vision. My grandfather had been a mason in Lebanon, and in America he owned his own lumberyard. He was extremely independent and could easily move around his workplace accomplishing the tasks that needed to be done.

Mrs. Georgia Joseph (center), her parents and siblings, 1921

It was very difficult for me to understand my grandfather's blindness. I strongly felt that if he was able to do so many things while blind, anyone could do anything. His favorite saying to me was "My eyes, come and take me." If he heard a person rattling a can for money, he immediately asked me to take a dollar from his pocket and deposit it in the can. He would do the same for all jingling cans of beggars he heard on the streets.

People often would ask what was wrong with my grandfather and I would respond by saying that "He's blind and cannot see." Their stares never bothered my grandfather but they surely made me more tolerant of challenged people. My grandfather thought that he was just the same as everyone else and his handicap was not an issue.

I feel that I was my "grandfather's eyes." If you truly care for someone, anything can be accomplished in life. I have great empathy for blind people because I feel they have missed so much because they cannot see. My grandfather, however, never complained of his blindness. He totally accepted his disability. God gave him a certain talent to do so many things and my grandfather was a living example of this.

I originally came to Detroit to help my sister. It was here that I met my husband, who also came from a loving family. We both tried to instill in our children the importance of family ties, hard work and the belief in God. I feel that these things are the keys to success. A person must not be afraid to get his hands dirty and must accept what life deals him. One must go forward and accept life's ups and downs. My 80th birthday was celebrated this year.

Mrs. Georgia Joseph, 75th birthday celebration, October 14, 1993

Mrs. Bernice Ash

"At my age life is drawing its curtain on me, but every day seems sweeter."

My father's mother, my grandmother, must have been the guiding light in my life. She was blind for 25 years and yet she learned the Bible by heart and became an ordained minister. Every summer she would come on the train, a three-day journey, to stay with us for the entire summer. All three children had to walk her to church every Sunday. It was a long walk and we had to watch very carefully that she did not stumble and fall. Every bump in the sidewalk had to be avoided. We really felt very important after we had arrived safely at the church and then again back home. She must have had great faith to be guided by three young children. I was the oldest at 9 years of age.

Right before going to bed, she would tell us the many wonderful stories from the Bible about Joseph and the many-colored coat, Noah and the ark he built, and many others. To this day I vividly remember these stories.

When I was in high school, I taught a Sunday school class. Today I am still very active in my church, holding any job that needs to be filled. Life is good. We have to accept it as it comes to us. Be happy with our family and friends. As friends move away or die, we must keep making new friends. At my age life is drawing its curtain on me, but every day seems sweeter. Every flower gives more pleasure. Every bird singing as the sun comes up lifts my spirit for the day. I feel blessed.

Mrs. Bernice Ash with doll dressed for Goodfellows and one of her handmade quilts, Christmas 1997

Mrs. Bernice Lezotte

"Bear ye one another's burdens."

I was born in Windsor, Ontario, Canada, and came to the Downriver area with my parents and older sister when I was 2 years old. A brother was later born here. None of my grandparents, aunts, uncles or cousins chose to follow us to the United States so we were raised without an extended family. All of my relatives are still in Canada or England. Being without family here, we made the church the center of our life for spiritual and social activities. As a young girl I belonged to a church group whose motto was "Bear ye one another's burdens" and that became my philosophy and aim in life.

I have been a caregiver most of my married life. My mother-in-law became a widow at the age of 66 and simply gave up any interest in life. My husband and I cared for all her needs until she died at the age of 89. Our middle son has Down syndrome. For the first eight years of his life, it was a struggle to keep him alive. During the past several years he has suffered from a severe heart problem and it is difficult to make him comfortable. His pediatrician when he was young allowed us to visit many parents of newborn Down syndrome children. We attempted to give them some insight into the problems and joys they would encounter in their child's life. It was a very rewarding experience. Throughout my son's life, we have been and continue to be active in the local and state Association for Retarded Citizens. These organizations brought us together with many caring and concerned parents trying to do their best for their children. Moreover, school and church afforded more care-giving activities to me. For the past two years since my husband's death, I have been volunteering for the hospice group that cared for him in his final days.

Music has also been a special gift in my life. I was awarded a high school letter for solo work. I still sing at weddings and funerals and am a member of my church choir. My mother and father sang in choirs and my father-in-law had a magnificent voice and sang for 40 years in his church. My husband was blessed with both an exceptional speaking and singing voice and sang in his church choir as well as producing a minstrel show in the early '50s. Although my husband and I were of different faiths and attended different churches, we always helped one another with various musical events as needed. Our youngest son enjoys playing the guitar and our oldest son, an attorney, has joined with several other attorney friends to produce musicals. They have performed all over the state of Michigan and elsewhere. I like to think that over the years we have been able to give many others pleasurable moments of inspiration and fun.

I have some treasured memories of the day my husband died. Although he had heart problems for 23 years, he died of cancer in four short months. The last five days my husband was under hospice care. The last two days they moved a hospital bed into our bedroom next to the double bed we had shared for the past 48-1/2 years. It was Super Bowl Sunday and our oldest grandson would come in and out of the bedroom reporting the scores to his grandpa. At one point our grandson and granddaughter, 5 and 2 years old at the time, were bouncing up and down on our double bed, and my little grandson, in a singsong voice, said, "Grandma is taking care of grandpa and we're keeping him company." And keep him company we did. The whole family was there until the moment of his death!

Looking back on all of this I am reminded of the last line of the Prayer of the Anonymous Confederate soldier which reads, "I am among all men most richly blessed."

Anonymous Patient

*"He said to me that the more you give to charities, church
or temples, the more you get in return. You must leave the
world a better place when you die."*

This is about my husband. His memory is a benediction of
himself. He was raised by parents who left Germany
because of the conditions in that country before World War II.
They were aware of trouble happening in their country. Their
goal was to either come to the U.S. or go to South America.
Because an aunt was already here and loved America, they
decided to join her. My husband always lived in a household of
eight or more people. His parents always had refugees from
Europe living in their home. My husband's family consisted of
two parents, four brothers, one sister and himself. He was the
youngest. They always had four to six other people sharing their
home, food and clothing. The families would stay about a year,
get a job, save some money and then move on. Meanwhile,
another family would arrive. They had only four bedrooms.
Each set of parents had a bedroom and the other two bedrooms
were assigned one for a girls' bedroom and the other for the
boys.

Through junior high school my husband shared a twin bed
with his brother. One slept at the top and the other at the bottom
of the bed. Finally in high school he had his own twin bed. His
brothers all joined the Army when they were through with

school. World War II was in progress. He thought nothing of it. Sharing was something he was brought up to do. Also his parents wanted the children to speak English and insisted on speaking it in the home. They were in United States now and it was important to speak English and not German.

When my husband joined the Army after high school, he was excited to be able to travel and serve his country. Also, living with many people together in a barracks made him feel right at home. Many of the other soldiers complained about sleeping in a big room with many other soldiers, so my husband would tell them he was used to it. They had their own bed and they shouldn't complain.

He was chosen to be in the Army band and went to Japan in 1948. In 1950 the Korean War broke out and he was one of the first solders to arrive in the beginning of July to fight the North Koreans. He was 35 miles from the Yule River in China when, on Thanksgiving Day, the Chinese Communists became involved and the soldiers had to retreat to the 38th parallel. He was lucky to survive. Many of his friends were captured and killed. When it was time for him to come home after serving his one year in Korea, President Truman made an order extending everyone's time in the service for another year so he was forced to stay in Korea. He made it home with many honors including the Bronze Star. He was very patriotic. Our big U.S. flag was always flown on holidays. About 20 soldiers he served with in Korea remained friends and we often had reunions. "A person becomes very close to people who lived in foxholes together," he would always say to me.

Upon his discharge from the Army he came home and started college. That's where I met him in an English class on Shakespeare. We fell in love. Neither set of parents was happy about us marrying each other. He was Jewish and I was Christian. This was a major problem for everyone except us. Forty-two years ago this was very unusual. We decided to celebrate all holidays with each family so no one would be hurt.

We had four children–two boys and two girls. Only the girls survived. He taught our girls that they were put on earth to make the world a better place in which to live and to benefit society. He always felt a parent should give his children confidence in themselves. He taught them when they were little that they must go to college and do their best in whatever they chose to do. Both of our girls are engineers. Both are doing very well.

My husband wrote short stories, poetry and children's stories. He oil painted, did watercolor, wrote music and lyrics. He played many instruments including the saxophone, clarinet, flute, organ, piano and guitar. He was very artistic and talented. His feeling was that everyone should leave the world a better place when they die. Moreover, my husband requested nothing for himself–no gifts etc., but always gave in return. He gave flowers, cards, poetry, gifts, and money to students and paid for dinners anonymously.

He was a member of the Masonic organization and worked with the youth groups in the state of Michigan. When someone needed money for tuition or books, he would always help. There were many times I would have money saved for something like a dishwasher or a microwave and it would disappear because some student needed help and the money was used for that person. He said to me that the more you give to charities, church or temples, the more you get in return. You must leave the world a better place when you die.

I was very ill many times during our marriage. I lost two babies, had blood clots and many surgeries, but he was always at my side encouraging me to get well. I became injured at work and he retired to be at home to help me. He made me get out of bed and get dressed every day and get moving. He took me to lunch, shop or just a walk around the block. Without his encouragement I would not have made it.

In the summer of 1996 he started having trouble with his stomach. He had a physical yearly so he thought it was something minor but it was cancer of the colon. The cancer had spread to his lymph nodes, liver and kidney. The doctors gave him only six weeks to six months to live. He ended up living a year and a half. He was on chemotherapy most of the time. He knew he was dying. There were many discussions on what to do after he was gone, such as what people and charities to give money to. He would tell me you have achieved success when you love, laugh and live well and leave children on earth to carry on.

He wrote a Christmas carol and gave it to my church in my honor. The church dedicated the song to him and sang it in church four days before he died. He heard it on a tape they made for him. It made him very happy. The song is beautiful. Both a Christian minister and a rabbi visited him in the hospital. They both prayed with him. His wish was to die at home but that is not what happened. The whole month of December 1997 he was in the hospital dying. I was there every day to try to encourage him to get better so he could come home. He wanted to have potato pancakes on Hanukkah but instead they had a respirator doing his breathing for him. He became better and the doctors took the respirator off on Tuesday afternoon–the beginning of Hanukkah. He said he would never have the respirator on him again.

The following day his breathing was more labored and the doctors wanted him to be put on the respirator again. He said no more life support machinery. He said he had enough and was ready to die. I stayed with him till the end, talking to him, holding his hand, petting him and telling him how much I loved him.

When my husband died, I kissed him goodbye, pulled away from him and at the same time a white smoke or white cloud left his head and body. The top of his bed was facing some black windows so it was very noticeable. I thought I was seeing something that wasn't there but the male nurse attending him also saw it. This had to be his spirit leaving him to go to Heaven. He died about six o'clock on Christmas morning on Jesus' birthday. He made it through his holiday and died on my holiday. I really felt comfort knowing he was in Heaven with God.

Because he died during the holidays we thought many people would not be at the funeral home. To my surprise, hundreds of people came and paid their respects to him and me. I have since received many letters from young people telling me how he had helped them either with advice, a few words of encouragement or money. The doctors who assisted him wrote letters telling me how much they admired him and would always remember him. After living with such a great man I could never marry again. I do not want anything but to be with him forever when I die.

Mr. Steve Ford

*"Three decades later, I said, that boy was a better man
for how Harry touched his life."*

As a journalist reporting in both the broadcast and print
media, my profession is to study, understand and reveal
what I discover to audiences I serve. Yet when it comes to life
experiences, my 41 years of observations leave me short of being
qualified to pass along the treasured reward of wisdom that
senior citizens gain in their journeys. Still, as the child of a
father who was a professor of sociology and a mother who was
an actress, I was taught early in life about the virtues of observing people–and remembering.

It is, therefore, in reflection about one person who has
touched my life that I recall the strong sense of humanity that I
realize we are all capable of conveying to each other. The
humanity I wish to highlight is in the form of a generous regard
for even the seemingly smallest of kind gestures to a child.

In marveling at the positive spirit that can be passed along in
the gift of an older person's kindness to a child, I regularly recall
a cherished memory of when I was just 6 years old. My father
had hired one of his university graduate students, who supported his family by working as a carpenter, to construct an
additional room on our family's home. The student, Harry Jurey,
was a middle-aged man of particular modesty.

What is notable about my memories of Harry is that from the first day that he worked to construct the addition to our home, he allowed me to follow him and ask questions throughout his daily work. As a curious and talkative youngster that I know I was, it still makes me pause to recall that he never lost patience with my eager fascination and probably constant inquiries about his work–from his supervising the massive truck and workers in the laying of the concrete foundation for the structure . . . to his detailed measuring, sawing and fabrication of the wood framing for the walls.

Mr. Steve Ford, 1998

While the memories of the series of days and weeks that I would come home from school with eager anticipation of joining Harry while he worked remain a bit hazy, there is one scene that I can remember with vivid recollection. One afternoon, Harry invited me to join him to take a mid-afternoon lunch break. There I sat by his side on a bench while he opened his metal lunch box. Out came the thermos, a hard-boiled egg, and then a sandwich wrapped in wax paper. As he began to eat, I remember he paused to look down at me and then he smiled as he reached into his lunch box for one small last item, also wrapped in wax paper. It was a large, round piece of chocolate candy.

Harry opened the wax paper to reveal the chocolate dessert that was apparently placed in the lunch box by his wife. What struck me with instant delight was that he offered the chocolate that was intended for his dessert as a joyous gesture to me. I gladly accepted the candy and promptly took a bite into the juicy morsel to discover that it was a chocolate-covered cherry. "Zowie," I thought to myself. "I've never had a chocolate-covered cherry! That's tasty!"

Harry successfully completed the addition to my family's home and years of my life seemed to quickly elapse forward from that moment in my childhood. Yet that experience remained a clear and fond memory. It wasn't until I was in my mid-30s that it dawned on me how significant Harry's gesture was. When he gave that little 6-year-old boy a chocolate cherry, he likely did not expect that child to recall the moment as an adult man more than 25 years later. That was the beauty, it occurred to me, of Harry's character and humanity.

Because my family remained in contact with Harry over the years, I took the opportunity to call him and his wife, Louise, one evening and asked if I could pay them a social visit. A few days later I arrived at their home and sat down with them in their living room. I proceeded to tell Harry and his wife the story about that 6-year-old boy who was so flattered and excited to be given a chocolate-covered cherry by that neat guy who was a carpenter on his family's house.

Then I opened up a paper bag and pulled out a gift-wrapped box and handed it to Harry, while his amused and proud wife watched us. Harry opened the box and found that it was filled with two dozen chocolate-covered cherries. I actually became a bit emotional, as did Harry, as I explained to him that the grown man who was bringing him those chocolates was really just that grateful little boy. I told him that I never forgot his kind gesture to me, and his friendship to that curious child . . . a boy he could have merely brushed off, but chose to treat with sensitive kindness.

I also told Harry that the lesson in life that he showed me was a gift that demonstrated how powerful the positive effect of caring for the feelings of a child can be. Harry had treated one little boy with warmth and generosity he could have only hoped that child would appreciate, and even more remotely, remember as an adult. Three decades later, I said, that boy was a better man for how Harry touched his life.

We don't always have a chance to come back and thank those who have been kind to us. Yet perhaps more importantly, we don't always know if the children we're kind to will remember the regard we offer them. Like Harry, however, I learned that when we give to a child, it is the model for the greatest giving of all.

Mrs. Betty Smith

"Doing God's work on earth."

I have been aware of the actions of many people in my life, but the one who made the greatest impression was Jesse, my best friend–my husband of 47 years.

He was a quiet man with a slight speech impediment, which did not prevent him from showing compassion for his fellow man. This was evident in the hours he spent helping hospitalized veterans, neighbors and family.

Because of him I have become a more thoughtful and caring person by doing for others. My philosophy is "Doing God's work on earth."

Two weeks before my husband's death I found the following prayer in my Bible–I know it tells what a "friend" I had.

I SAID A PRAYER FOR YOU TODAY

I said a prayer for you today and know God
must have heard. I felt the answer in my heart
although He spoke no word.

I didn't ask for wealth or fame. I knew you
wouldn't mind.

I asked Him to send treasures of a far more
lasting kind. I asked that He'd be near you
at the start of each new day.

To grant you health and blessings and friends
to share your way. I asked for happiness for
you in all things great and small, but it was for
His loving care I prayed for most of all.

This prayer was read at his funeral by our minister. Six
months after Jesse's death, I returned to school and graduated in
1996 with a degree in Gerontology at the age of 71. At the present time I do volunteer work at the Veterans Hospital in Allen
Park one morning a week. On Wednesdays I am a facilitator for
a Senior Citizen Grief Support Group that meets in Dearborn
Heights.

I am grateful that I can continue to serve God and my fellow
man.

*Betty and Jesse Smith attend Harvest Dinner
at church, 1993*

Mrs. Marianne Glinn

"Our captain received two SOS calls from ships, but it was too late to save them."

Seeing the movie "Titanic" recently stirred up a lot of horrific memories for me. In 1929 when I was 6 years old, my parents came from Germany on a ship called *Bremen*, which claimed to be the largest steamship in the world.

We left Bremerhaven in December, the first Sunday in Advent, and ran into the worst storm in 40 years–a hurricane. Our captain disobeyed orders to return, claiming he could make the trip in three days. (It took 13.) I found out since that many prayers were said for our small family, both in that small village in Germany and also in the U.S.

The papers were filled with articles about the ship in distress. Our captain received two SOS calls from ships, but it was too late to save them. Our cabin filled with water to the point that we had to move in with another family.

This experience so affected my life that to this day I will not go on a ship where I cannot see both shores. I also have often wondered why the Lord spared us and for what purpose. It truly strengthened my faith in Him. Also, why were we spared the terrible times people went through in Germany during World War II? That question was made clear to me recently after a visit from a German cousin.

Mrs. Marianne Glinn, childhood photo, 1930

I had very God-fearing parents for whom I am deeply grateful and always tried to instill that faith in my children and grand-children. It seems that whatever trials and tribulations life deals us, the Lord is there with us and we are never alone.

Although my parents are both gone now, I'll never forget what a great influence they had on my life and how much help they were to me and my family when my marriage broke up. Also, Dr. Ulrich was a wonderful help and confidant during those try-ing times. I will never forget him and how he helped me make many wise decisions, particularly concerning my youngest son, whom I had to raise alone. I often think the rare affliction I had at that time was for a purpose. Otherwise, I never would have met Dr. Ulrich. The Lord works in mysterious ways.

❖

Mr. Charles Hambel

"This man is caring, so put him in the Medical Corps."

My road to life started by coming from a very poor family of 11 children. I was the second eldest. Growing up back then was very difficult with little money and material things. We managed to do OK. No one, however, told me I was going to be the caregiver for my mother.

Our home had no bath or running water, so I did all the carrying of water to our home. I did this for many years until we were able to move to better surroundings. I graduated from high school, but was unable to go to college. I secured several jobs until I was finally drafted into the U.S. Army and experienced all the "goodies" of basic training, etc. It seems God said to the Army, "This man is caring, so put him in the Medical Corps." They did, and I served in Korea for two years, tending to the wounded.

After my career in the service for two years, I returned home safe and sound and resided in Ohio for about four years. I then relocated to Michigan, married and started my banking career. I received assistance from a friend of my wife's family. I could see and really watched how this friend loved and cared for his customers. This was "right up my alley" because I loved to help everyone. I continue to always go out of my way to help others.

The following story now comes to mind. When I became a bank branch manager several years later, a male customer came to the door of the bank. This was before we were open in the morning. I went to the door and asked him what he wanted and he said he needed to get a haircut. He seemed very sad. I said to him, "Let me give you the money." He returned later and was so happy. To this day, I still love to be of help to anyone in need. I know God had plans 13 years ago as he put his loving hands on me and I survived a bout with cancer.

Mr. Charles Hambel in Japan en route to Korea, 1951

✦

Mrs. Isabelle McCarthy

"Do everything you can to solve your problem and then turn the problem over to God."

I don't seem to be able to pinpoint any one person or event that shaped my philosophy of life. Rather, I feel it was derived from my environment. I came from a family of four–a mother, a father and an older sister. I was raised in a Christian atmosphere both at home and in school. Through the years I have had a good marriage, eight children and 22 grandchildren. Moreover, I've developed a strong faith in God, and have tried to be a follower of His Ten Commandments.

One thing I have found to be very successful in my life: "Ask and you shall receive." When troubled and in doubt, my mind flustered, I ask God to help me make the right decision. Sometimes waiting for discernment requires patience. However, when the time comes that a decision or necessary action must be taken, I find I have reached a determination, an answer to the problem and always satisfying in the sense that I feel peaceful about it. The philosophy here may be "Do everything you can to solve your problem and then turn the problem over to God." It works for me and is very comforting.

My feelings regarding death are that even though my husband is now deceased after 48 years of marriage and I live alone, I will always enjoy the company of our Lord. What makes the death of a loved one or the thought of one's own death bearable is the belief in eternal life. The following is a prayer that I try to say daily. It seems to encompass so much that it can possibly be considered the embodiment of Christian principles.

Lord, Make Me an Instrument of Thy Peace

Where there is hatred, let me sow love;
Where there is injury, pardon;
Where there is doubt, faith;
Where there is darkness, light;
And where there is sadness, joy.

O Divine Master, grant that I may not
so much seek to be consoled as to console;
To be understood as to understand;
To be loved, as to love;
For it is in giving that we receive;
It is in pardoning that we are pardoned;
And it is in dying that we are born to eternal life.

– Saint Francis of Assisi

Robert and Isabelle McCarthy, 50th high school class reunion, 1995

Mrs. Ann Zelenak

"Annie, you made my day!"

My personal philosophy has always been compassion for the lonely and the handicapped.

A simple phone call is all it took to make one of the former members of our senior group so happy. Due to illness, she was unable to attend any more of our meetings. How lonely she became!

The telephone was her lifeline, so to speak. She'd call and talk she did. Our conversations were at least one hour minimum. Then I would call and she would say, "Annie, you made my day!" I do not receive many phone calls myself. I would mention at our meetings about how a simple phone call to this lady would be so welcome. The few members who did call her said the conversation was too long. She also would repeat things, which was true. No compassion here.

She passed away recently and I have never regretted the many times we talked, even though it wasn't always convenient for me. While she lived, I tried to make her part of our lives.

❖

❖

Mr. & Mrs. Swanson

*Trust in the Lord with all your heart and lean not on
your own understanding; in all your ways acknowledge
Him and He will make your paths straight.*
                        – Proverbs 3:5 & 6 NIV

Our philosophy on how we approach life was formed in our
childhood through our parents' belief in one God, the creator of the universe, revealed in the Bible as the source of all
truth for living. Through experiences growing up, we had
opportunities to examine this point of view for ourselves and
concluded it was the right path to take.

When we met in our early 20s, our faith was the foundation
for our individual lives and subsequently our married life
together. It has guided us through 50 years of marriage and parenting and we have never regretted our commitment to our bib-
lical faith. When problems inevitably arose, we had in common
the source of wisdom to find our way through them.

We also believe in remembering to be grateful for blessings in
life. We are particularly thankful for our children and grandchildren and the joy and love they bring. We also developed many
strong friendships through the years. Our friends have been with
us through good times and bad and their concern, prayers and
genuine care have been invaluable additions to our lives.

Three passages in the Bible have been especially meaningful
in guiding our path through life. They have provided us with
direction, wisdom and a sense of purpose throughout the years.

Marjorie and Walter Swanson, California, 1997

Two verses come from the Old Testament and the third verse is found in the New Testament.

> Trust in the Lord with all your heart and lean not on your own understanding; in all your ways acknowledge Him and He will make your paths straight.
>
> – Proverbs 3:5 & 6 NIV

> Remember your Creator in the days of your youth, before the days of trouble come and the years approach when you will say, "I find no pleasure in them."
>
> – Ecclesiastes 12:1 NIV

> We know that in everything God works for good, with those who love Him, who are called according to His purpose.
>
> – Romans 8:28 RSV

Mrs. Dorothy Mundle

"I am still learning and seeking."

I have been surrounded by good people all my life–my parents, my two sisters, my husband and my children. I was born in Carleton, Michigan, in 1919. After high school, I graduated from business college. I married when I was 21. Ron and I had three children, two of whom preceded us in death–Linda and Roland Jr. Valerie is a blessing in our life. I have two beloved grandchildren, Anna and Joe. My dear husband died in 1996, after a long battle with Parkinson's disease. I am alone now for the first time in my life. I am living in an apartment in a retirement village. Life is like a roller coaster ride, with many ups and downs.

I remember two turning points in my life. First, when I was in my mid-30s while sweeping the kitchen floor, I thought, "I sweep this floor today and tomorrow I must sweep it again. Is this what life is about?" Then in my 60s while attending a Bible class, the teacher mentioned John 5:24: "I tell you the truth, whoever hears my words and believes Him who sent me has eternal life, and will not be condemned; he has crossed over from death to life." I realized I did not need to die to have eternal life. It was mine now. What a comfort.

I am still learning and seeking. However, some thoughts have sustained me over the years. I am God's child and everyone I meet is a child of God. I need to have a church family. I try to live by the Golden Rule. I try to be optimistic and look on the bright side. Money and books are just paper if not shared. Before I can help someone, I must have my own house in order. As I grow older, I find myself seeking to accept, rather than to understand. I am grateful for the privilege of a lifetime on God's beautiful planet.

Ron and Dot Mundle, 1989

Mr. Keith Harkins

"So I'll be a kid at heart and live each day as if it is my last."

I grew up in Western Kentucky. What is my philosophy of life? I'm not really sure. The first thing that comes to mind is when I was a little boy my mom let me paint my bedroom furniture. On the back of the chest of drawers I wrote, "Never give up no matter what." This has helped me get through many hard times. I truly never give up no matter what.

At the age of 30 I lost my best friend of 20 years. I thought my heart would break. Knowing that there was something that I must learn from this, I knew that I must move on and not live in the past. Today, because of Greg's death, I look at each and every day as a gift from God.

Although I'm not sure that there is a proper way to pray, I like to get down on my knees and thank God for every day He has given me. For today, I have learned to take full responsibility for my mistakes, deal with them and focus on today. The truth is that we can only count on today. Yesterday has passed and tomorrow may never come. So I'll be a kid at heart and live each day as if it is my last.

❖

Mr. Keith Harkins, 1997

Mr. Milo Teer

"I make other transplant patients realize that they are not alone."

I started as a patient with Dr. Ulrich in 1970. I was always impressed with the manner in which he treated all his patients. He was never in a hurry and always took time to talk to you. Every office visit would start with "How are you?" to my wife, our son and me. At each subsequent visit, Dr. Ulrich always remembered what I had told him about my family's activities on my previous visit. In all of our talks he never failed to say, "Praise God" or "Thank God," and he would always end our visit with "God bless you."

I remember when Dr. Ulrich told me he was getting ready to retire and was looking for a replacement. I was confident he would leave his patients in good hands. I met Dr. Waldinger during an appointment in 1985. I still remember coming home and telling my wife that Dr. Ulrich had found a doctor just like him to take over his dermatological practice.

All was good in my life—a good marriage, a nice son, a great job and good health. As time passed, however, I found I couldn't finish my daily three-mile run, an activity I enjoyed every morning. In just a little over a week's time I saw my internist, who said I should consult a heart specialist. The heart doctor told me that my heart was double its normal size as a result of a heart

Mr. Milo Teer, Transplant Olympics - 400 yard dash, 1998

disease called cardiomyopathy. I was sent home with little hope and told to get my things in order. This took place in the summer of 1981. The doctor's advice was very close to the truth.

During the next two years, my health deteriorated quickly. I was admitted into the hospital for congestive heart failure on several occasions. At the beginning of 1984, I grew steadily worse. Two heart specialists at the University of Michigan Hospital told my wife and me that my only hope was a heart transplant. A call was received on April 30, 1984, that a heart had been located for me. On May 1, 1984, I received my heart transplant.

Many friends have asked how I was able to cope with the turn of events in my life. I had been in and out of the hospital for two years, received a heart transplant and yet was uncertain about what the future had in store for me. I can, however, think of many reasons why I am a survivor. The primary reason was my faith in God and completely trusting in Him. My faith carried me through the first 38 years of my life and why shouldn't it carry me through my remaining years? I really believe that He will not bestow upon me more than I am able to handle. We are never to question what He sends our way. Before and during all my medical procedures, I say my prayers. I pray that He will give me the strength to accept His will. When I pray, I always include a prayer for my doctors. I ask that God will guide their hands and bless them for their dedication to their patients. Along with my faith in God is my complete trust in my doctors.

I've encountered other medical problems since my heart transplant, mainly skin cancer and a serious vascular disease which affects my legs. I am very lucky that my doctors are so dedicated in treating my physical problems, but also are truly concerned with the quality of my life. I try not to dwell on my problems but rather focus on all the good things in my life. I hope that I'm a good role model, especially to transplant recipients. I make other transplant patients realize they are not alone.

Mrs. Marie Licari

"She said to me, 'Marie, live your life to the fullest.'"

There are many philosophies that I live by but this one is by far the most important to me. My philosophy is to live life to the fullest.

In 1964, I was faced with a divorce and received custody of my five children. At that time, women's wages were not what they are today. Therefore, my children and I struggled greatly.

In my Golden Years with 16 grandchildren and five great-grandchildren so far, I am hopefully wiser. Life experiences of being a single parent and raising children alone taught me to always put God first. He has much to do with survival. Live your life to the fullest each day.

When I moved to Taylor, Michigan, I felt very low and depressed. I usually went to church every Sunday. After my move, I became involved with a church. There was a nun at the church who understood my feelings and got me involved in working at a nursing home as part of the Christian Service Commission. She said to me, "Marie, live your life to the fullest." I now do this, and as a result have become more religious. This has developed a deeper love for God. This particular person helped to form my philosophy of life. We still often have lunch together.

Mrs. Marie Licari (left) with Sister Jean Horger, 1999

Mrs. Ruth Schlesser

"We are so grateful for these long-standing 'ties that bind.'"

From the time I was a little child, my mother read to me frequently–mainly Bible stories from the Old and New
Testaments. When I grew a little older I attended Sunday school
faithfully each week and heard again many of the same stories
told by dedicated, caring Sunday school teachers, pastors and
youth leaders.

My dad and mother and I attended the church as a family.
When I learned to play the piano, I was able to play for Sunday
school and church services and later for the choir, using the
piano and finally a newly installed organ.

This inner-city church has seen a number of pastors and
members come and go, and many other changes have taken
place. However, long-ago members and friends still keep in
touch and get together from time to time. We are so grateful for
these long-standing "ties that bind."

Would you believe, at age 71, I am still there–praising, praying and playing–thanks be to God!

❖

Mr. Robert Fink

"All things come from God"

I was the only child of a beautiful young woman from Kentucky and a high-strung father from Illinois. Born in southwest Detroit in 1929, I had the wonderful experience of growing up with grandma, grandpa, two aunts, two uncles, mom and dad in a two-story, one-bath house. My mom and dad and I lived upstairs and grandma and grandpa downstairs. (I lived downstairs most of the time.) The neighborhood was a diverse melding of nationalities.

Growing up, I really enjoyed watching my grandma make bread and cook. In the late summer, trips to a farm market were the beginning of the canning season. All kinds of fruits and vegetables were canned. Everyone was involved. One of the things I still do to this day is chop my own cabbage for sauerkraut. I would also help braid rag rugs and played under the quilting frame (made by my dad) as my grandma and mother quilted.

My grandma's small bedroom off the kitchen was a place of pure ecstasy. Her bed was a homemade feather bed. What a joy it was to jump on the bed and sleep with grandma. I started going to church with her at an early age. She would read stories to me from the Bible and quote scriptures from it on

Mr. Robert Fink, Chicago World's Fair, 1933

many subjects. She made sure I learned one verse a week for Sunday school. As I sit here today and think about her, I realize what a profound impact she had on my outlook on life. "All things come from God."

I am happy to be able to tell my grandchildren stories of the summers I spent on my great-aunt's farm in Illinois as a young boy–the nights with kerosene lamps, hand-cranked telephones, gasoline washing machines, drawing water from a cistern, slopping the hogs, gathering the eggs in the hen house and catching a chicken for dinner for my aunt. She would wring its neck, feather and clean it. Years later my wife witnessed such an event and could not eat the chicken for dinner. My Aunt Tess, with whom I stayed those summers, was my grandma's sister and she was also a very religious woman. Her many prayers and blessings will always be remembered by me.

I must tell you of an experience that revealed to me the power of having a strong faith in the healing power of the Lord Jesus Christ. As a young man I had Meniere's disease, a condition which affects the inner ear. This lasted about five years. It left me totally immobile for as long as 48 hours or more at times. My Aunt Tess came to Michigan to visit that summer. No sooner had she seen me sick in bed, she was on her knees praying with a hand on my head. Through my faith and Jesus' healing power, my dizziness has not returned. "Wait on the Lord."

What a beautiful family I am blessed with now. My wife, Phyllis (we met in high school), and I have three wonderful sons. We waited 11 years for our first grandchild. A lovely lady reminded me to be patient. We are now blessed with seven beautiful grandchildren–three boys and four girls. When my three sons were growing up, I wanted them to learn to play a musical instrument, but they had no desire. I had studied music for many years, playing in schools, churches, weddings and concerts. Now, years later, I'm able to hear my grandsons play the clarinet, French horn and trumpet in concerts and see my granddaughters in their dance recitals.

The past 49 years have been with a person of unending love. She has always been there for me, especially the last seven months during my chemotherapy. Our life together has been, and will continue to be, a time of great joy and love and the giving of our friendship to others.

Mr. Ray Wolfe

"For God, all things are possible."

A man was shot in the head. As a lay chaplain, I have had a number of unusual experiences that illustrate that with God all things are possible.

I was visiting with a young man who had been shot in the head while attending a social event. He was not the target of the shooter. Steve had a grazing wound and was getting well.

In the course of several visits, I met his mother and grandmother who informed me that he was attending college and had good spiritual values and support. We prayed that God would heal him soon and he could complete his education.

Several weeks after his discharge, he was back in the hospital, much to my surprise. "Steve," I said, "how are you doing?" He replied, "I'm not sure. I have had blinding headaches for over a week. The doctors have examined me thoroughly and can't find any physical cause." "Well," I said, "just the thought of being shot in the side of the head would give me a headache. It's a traumatic experience. Your denomination is Catholic and your parents tell me you have strong spiritual values. Do you believe you can be healed through prayer?" Without hesitation, Steve said, "Yes, I do." As he sat on the edge of his bed, I stood before him and explained: "Steve, there are no guarantees. Nothing may happen, you may get well today, or it may take weeks or months."

As he sat on the bed, I stood in front of him and for some reason placed my hands with my palms over his eyes and fingers covering his temples. I said a brief extemporaneous prayer and removed my hands from him, really not knowing what to expect. "You won't believe this," Steve said. "My headache is gone." We thanked God in joint prayer and I left.

The lesson I learned from this was, "Don't sell prayer short." For Matthew 19:26 says, "For God, all things are possible." You see, I wasn't expecting such immediate results. God has His own way of doing things.

Mr. Ray Wolfe, Grand Teton National Park, Wyoming, 1990

Mr. Jack Stead

"People I don't know, and unable to speak their language, gave me food, clothes, shelter, transportation and a route over the mountains to Spain."

I was shot down during the war and here is my offering.

The plane takes off. It is 7:40 a.m., 13th Mission, Rattlesden, England, April 27, 1944. I was still a boy, married, new daughter, but still a boy. Now I have grown up quickly. Life used to seem long, but now each day seemed as though it was going to be short.

This was to be an easy mission, back to base in four hours. Just over to France, drop bombs and return home.

We are hit with flak, on fire and falling. Bombs still aboard, we bail out. I hide and escape capture.

People I don't know, and unable to speak their language, gave me food, clothes, shelter, transportation and a route over the mountains to Spain. I was free, alive and can go home. Of all those who helped me, I only remember two.

So, from that day on I considered each day a special gift and each person someone to help if they needed it. I never could repay those I really owed. I have had a wonderful life and enjoyed everything I have been able to do for other people.

Mr. Jack Stead, Air Corps Staff Sergeant, home on leave, 1944

The following is from a newspaper report in 1944:

SAFE

Staff Sergeant Jack. W. Stead, 23, Fortress gunner, escaped via underground by walking several hundred miles after being shot down over France, April 27, 1944.

❖

Mr. Carl Bissinger

"I was young at the time but this experience and several others less threatening brought me to the realization that life is indeed fragile."

It was early in the morning on a cloudy but warm fall day. The year 1944; the place somewhere in central Germany. Our infantry platoon was ordered to dig-in about 200 yards from a farmhouse reported to be a German command post. We were deployed along a hedgerow, along a pile of firewood and a dilapidated shed used to house cattle. I was fortunate to be assigned a spot in the shed, which seemed at the time to offer the most protection from enemy gunfire.

I finished digging my ground cover, put my backpack just outside and crawled in to rest before our hot meal would be served. Within a matter of minutes, we came under a severe mortar attack. There was no place to run or hide so our only alternative was to hug the ground and pray. A shell landed within three feet of my position and a subsequent concussion literally lifted me about a foot from my foxhole. When the shelling stopped, I reached for my backpack to check for damage. There was nothing left but a small piece of burning canvas. I was young at the time but this experience and several others less threatening brought me to the realization that life is indeed fragile.

When the war ended, I returned home to renew a friendship with a lovely young lady who had served four years as a nurse's aide at a veterans hospital. She too had seen the high price many of our military had paid for our victory. When we married, we shared a similar appreciation of how true happiness can be found in the many things the Creator has provided—the flowers, the trees, the rain and all the animals—large and small.

Mr. Carl Bissinger, 78th Infantry Division, Berlin, 1945

Mr. Joe Lee Robbins

"Why I am who I am."

My high school American history teacher greatly admired
Abraham Lincoln, who once said, "All that I am or ever
hope to be, I owe to my darling mother." That caused me to
begin to reflect on how much I owed to my wonderful mother to
whom I was so close. This closeness continued through high
school, college, World War II, my marriage, and the rest of her
life.

Our letters to each other were always very tender and touching. We cherished every opportunity we could get to talk to each
other. Each one was always too short. She dearly, dearly loved
my daddy and all of us children. I was the oldest of six, three
boys and three girls.

When I was 6 years old, my 4-year-old brother Billy and I
stood on the bank of a mountain stream and watched as our
mother and daddy were baptized into the membership of the
Primitive Baptist Church in 1929. After that, we were taken to
church regularly. My mother was never happier than when some
of the church folks, especially the preachers, would come home
with us and eat and stay all night. She delighted in talking end-
lessly with them about the Bible and the life of the church and
its doctrine. Even after the company left, she would have daddy

Mr. Joe Lee Robbins, Aviation Cadet, Army Air Force, San Antonio, Texas, 1945

sit down and tell her everything that he had talked about with them when she had to be out of earshot back in the kitchen preparing the meals.

She, along with daddy, greatly encouraged us in our school-work. As a result, all of us except one became college graduates.

They counseled us regularly on what good behavior meant and insisted that we "be good." She would say, "Now, Joe Lee, you are the oldest. The others will look up to you and I want you to set a good example for them. You know what certain other boys are doing that we don't like. We don't want you doing any of those things." You can imagine the positive reinforcement that was applied when necessary to insure that these teachings were followed! Daddy was a coal miner in Harlan County, Kentucky. He made a good living for us, and we never ran out of food, even in the Depression. Mother was very resourceful in preparing very nutritious and inexpensive meals. I still love her staples: bean soup, corn bread, fried potatoes, biscuits, oatmeal, flour gravy, fried bacon and, of course, all of the fruits and veg-etables from the garden in their season.

She did all of this in houses with no running water, no refrig-erator and no inside toilet. We lived in a very old farmhouse on a 200-acre farm from 1938 to 1944 with no electricity, and water was drawn from a dug well. Largely due to her efforts, these were among the happiest years of our lives. I still remember the hymns I learned from listening to her sing as she did her work around the house and in the garden.

We identified with General Eisenhower who said they were poor but didn't know it when they grew up on a farm in Kansas. Our parents were always able to give us something for Christmas. We played with some kids who didn't get anything.

I wanted to play on the football team in high school, but daddy wouldn't let me. He let me play basketball. One day, when daddy and I were watching mother milk our cow, I asked him again to let me play football. He didn't say anything for a while, and then he said, "Joe Lee, do you see what a fine milk cow that 'Old Jerz' is?" I replied, "Of course I do. She gives us six gallons of milk a day and is as pretty as she can be!" He continued, "Do you think I would let her get all banged up and bruised playing football?" "No, sir!" I acknowledged. He explained, "Well, you know that I love you a whole lot more than I do this cow!" This story further represents the kind of wisdom that surrounded me while I was raised by this godly father and mother in the hills of Kentucky.

Daddy went to heaven in 1967 and mother in 1973. I still feel a wonderful warmth in my heart as I reminisce about them and the good hugs that we exchanged every time we were together.

I graduated from the University of Kentucky in 1947 with a Bachelor of Science Degree in Metallurgical Engineering. I worked for three years as a metallurgist for Revere Copper and Brass in Detroit, then five years as general foreman of the rolling mill. I then worked for 30 years for Ford as a project engineer and was part of the management team of Ford Motor Company's Rouge Steel Mill in Dearborn, Michigan.

I have also been blessed by the godly influences of both my first and second wives, with whom I have three children and two stepchildren. We have been active in the Lord's work as Sunday school teachers, singers, youth workers, deacons, and I as an elder. I also helped organize the Downriver Detroit Christian Businessmen's Committee in 1967. This group held regular luncheon and dinner meetings where men told how they had accepted Jesus as their Savior and Lord, and then invited the guests to accept Him also. My dermatologist, Dr. John Ulrich, spoke at several of these meetings.

After looking for many years for a Bible verse that seemed to explain, "Why I am who I am," I selected Galatians 6:14: "But may it never be that I should boast except in the cross of Lord Jesus Christ, by which the world has been crucified to me and I to the world."

Mrs. Jean Van Faasen

"The years have accumulated and so has the peace."

With the gift of seniority in years, we often find the answers to questions we asked in earlier life situations and can say, "Now I understand." My life did not follow a path I would have chosen. I would have selected a route devoid of troubles and ills with happy progress markers all along the way. Life is rarely so trouble free.

Major and minor detours occurred on my path, requiring great personal introspection and acceptance of situations I could not change. As I struggled against the changes, it was a turmoil I could not, or did not, share with others. My questioning was endless and without answers.

Realizing I was being forced to return to a career that I had happily abandoned to raise a family, I timidly approached combining a career and responsibilities of home. The challenges continued and increased, but amazingly so did my strengths. Along the way, I learned I could share my strengths with others as I often sensed the turmoil they masked behind their response of "I'm fine, thank you." Life prodded me and molded me to try harder, look deeper, be more understanding, and recognize the often difficult paths others are traveling.

Now I understand what life was trying to teach me and I am grateful for the passage, though rough at times. The years have accumulated and so has the peace. It is a lovely gift.

Mrs. Jean Van Faasen, 1996

Mrs. June Witthoff

*"I feel each hard time and sad time helped me to be
a stronger person."*

I was born in Sandwich (now Windsor), Ontario, Canada, on
June 5, 1917. I am the first born of five children. My mother
was a lovely, gentle woman and my father was a very intelligent,
rather stern, but kind man.

I grew up in the best of times. As children we were free to run
and play, without the restriction of fear, all through our neighborhood with other children who came from similar families.
The friends I had during those years are still friends to this day.

The Great Depression was a factor in our growing up. We had
very little money, which didn't bother us as children. Of course,
our friends also had very little money. We were all in the same
circumstances and enjoyed simple and inexpensive pleasures
together. This time in my life impressed on me the value of family, relationships and people. We were not able to focus on material things for happiness. I learned our true needs were really
few but always met. There was not any money for higher education after high school. It was hard to find employment, but luckily a friend of my dad's found a place for me to work in his business, so I went to work at 18 and worked until I met and married
my first husband, the father of my two very special sons. My
husband died at a very young age and didn't live long enough to

Mrs. June Witthoff, high school graduation, 1934

see how well his sons turned out. I am very proud of them and their wonderful families. I have grandchildren whom I love dearly.

After 11 years of widowhood, I married my present husband, Will, a fine and gentle man. We have been very fortunate to have traveled extensively in this country as well as Canada, the British Isles, Europe and Asia.

I am now living quietly with my husband of 21 years. We have a closeness with my sister and her husband, many dinners and excursions together, many family gatherings with nieces and nephews and visits with my children and their families.

I have had a very good life with many ups and downs, good times and hard times. I feel each hard time and sad time helped me to be a stronger person. I have a strong faith in God and I believe in the power of love.

Commentary:

Mrs. June Witthoff always greets me with kindness and a smile. Her wisdom has great meaning to me and can help us not only in our daily lives, but also in times of need and in guiding our children. Mrs. Witthoff writes, "I learned our true needs were really few but always met."

In *When Bad Things Happen to Good People*, Harold S. Kushner amplifies this concept when he writes,

> ". . .People who pray for miracles usually don't get miracles, any more than children who pray for bicycles, good grades, or boyfriends get them as a result of praying. But people who pray for courage, for strength to bear the unbearable, for the grace to remember what they have left instead of what they have lost, very often find their prayers answered. They discover that they have more strength, more courage than they ever knew themselves to have. Where do they get it? I would like to think that their prayers helped them find that strength. . . ."

❖

Mrs. Olive Sherby

"It has been said that life is a like a road well traveled with many risks. Many have traveled it before me and many will travel it after me. Those who have taken that road leave many lasting lessons we can glean from."

I was born May Olive Love in 1921–the middle child of five–all born in Canada. When I was 5 years old, my parents, like many from other countries, saw there were many more opportunities in the United States and so became U. S. citizens.

My childhood was a very happy one. I enjoyed school very much. The "Five Little Loves" grew close. My siblings were and are still very special to me. June, the first born in 1917, was beautiful and tall. We always looked to her as the big sister.

I remember as a schoolgirl and going to high school that I always loved June's beautiful blue sweater. Because she went to school earlier than I did, I borrowed that sweater one day and returned it before she got home, carefully folding and returning it to her dresser. But somehow she knew. I guess I looked guilty.

My brother John (1919-1985) came next. He was a very handsome young man and very popular with the girls. He became an Eagle Scout. I remember my mother pinning his badge on his uniform at a special ceremony. He was an outstanding trumpet player and received a scholarship to Wayne State University to play in the university band. He also served in the Army in Okinawa during World War II. A sudden heart attack took his life in 1985.

Mrs. Olive Sherby, 1945

I was the entertainer in our family. I tap danced, sang in the high school chorus and trio, sang with the dance band at school dances, and had the lead in the senior play. I was recognized at graduation as having never been absent or tardy through my entire 12 years of school.

In 1924, brother Robert was born. He became a very popular dentist, practicing for 40 years, and served in Korea in a M.A.S.H. unit as a dentist. He married his high school sweetheart.

Irene (1926-1996), our baby sister, was affectionately known as "Irene the Village Queen." She had deep brown eyes and black curly hair. She could do almost anything. She and I were kindred spirits and good friends. We shared secrets throughout our lives. We also shared clothes and hair curlers. Because we had only one set, she used them in the early evening and, before I went to bed, she had to surrender the curlers to me. Irene suffered terribly with painful rheumatoid arthritis. We miss Irene and John very much.

It has been said that life is like a road well traveled with many risks. Many have traveled it before me and many will travel it after me. Those who have taken that road leave many lasting lessons we can glean from.

In my own personal life, my dear sister who died last year left a legacy of the example of hope and a positive life. She struggled with the pain of crippling rheumatoid arthritis and chronic bronchiectasis, a disease of the bronchial tubes, which compromised her breathing, necessitating the use of 24-hour oxygen. Her husband of 50 years displayed true endless love for her as he cared for her every need. Together they kept a positive faith in God and in each other and always encouraged others, family and strangers.

There were many roadblocks with emergencies and surgeries. Her husband is a distance runner, who ran at early dawn while she was resting with the aid of oxygen. I suspect it was part of God's plan to keep his 74-year-old body well so he could be there to care for her.

Life continues to be a risky road, but I believe it is worth the risk. Because each day is a new beginning, the road does rise up and meets us even as we plan the trip. We need guidance and hope with no guarantee.

Regardless, prayerful life and love are worth the risk.

Commentary:

Mrs. Olive Sherby, the sister of Mrs. June Witthoff, greets me with kindness and a smile at each visit as well. It is always special for me when I am able to see family members. Mrs. Sherby, I have enjoyed meeting your children and grandchildren. Your entire family has enhanced my life.

Mrs. Sherby writes: "Life continues to be a risky road, but I believe it is worth the risk. Because each day is a new beginning, the road does rise up and meets us even as we plan the trip. We need guidance and hope with no guarantee. Regardless, prayerful life and love are worth the risk."

> I lift mine eyes to the hills,
> From where does my help come?
> My help comes from the Lord,
> Maker of Heaven and earth.
>
> – Psalm 121:1–2

Doug and Olive Sherby, 1985

Mr. Dale Anderson

"Even for the highest posts it is only in some cases application that is wanting, rarely the talent."

I think that it is fundamentally true that much important wisdom is acquired prior to school age. Unquestionably, the most significant values in my own life certainly were acquired at a very early age. In trying to remember life's earliest influences, I recall two little stories that my mother, at my insistence, would read to me over and over.

The first story was *The Little Red Hen*. This is a story of talking farm animals who taught others the wisdom that we must take responsibility for our own actions. The second meaningful story was entitled *The Little Engine that Could*. A small train engine in this book teaches that when we face up to our responsibilities by thinking positively, anything is possible. "I think I can, I think I can. . . ."

Although it probably was not recognized among the earliest lessons learned, I have come to realize that the most important possession that anyone has is his or her character or name. It takes a long, long time to build a good character, but only seconds to destroy it. Good character will carry you to a satisfying life and is something that no one can take away without your cooperation. Character is built, bit by bit, in your day-to-day dealings with other people and with yourself. It depends upon

Mr. Dale Anderson, weekly 75-mile ride in desert, Arizona, 1998

being honest and fair with others and with yourself. It requires that you respect other people, even if you do not like them. And it requires that you put forth your full effort and talents when given a job to do, whether or not someone is watching over you and whether or not you will receive a reward for completing the job.

Here are some helpful sayings and guidelines that, when conscientiously applied, will help us to acquire good character:

- Tell the Truth
- Cleanliness is Next to Godliness
- Finish What You Start
- Anything Worth Doing is Worth Doing Well
- Give the Benefit of the Doubt
- Don't Litter Your Mind or Your Environment
- All Work and No Play Make Jack a Dull Boy
- Live According to The Ten Commandments and The Golden Rule
- Stabilize Your Life With a Spiritual Anchor
- Practice Self-Discipline

A final piece of character-building wisdom was passed on to me in college by a mathematics professor who daily posted inspirational writings or quotes on the board. It is titled *Application and Ability*. This writing emphasizes that there is no attaining eminence without both, and where they unite, there is the greatest eminence. Mediocrity obtains more with application than superiority without. Work is the price that is paid for reputation. What costs little has little worth. Even for the highest posts it is only in some cases application that is wanting, rarely the talent.

Commentary:

When our children were in elementary school, Marcy and I would read *Teaching Your Children Values* by Linda and Richard Eyre at Sunday supper. This book was an excellent guide to help us instill values that would help our children throughout their lives. Linda and Richard Eyre write:

> "What do we owe a child?
> Sustenance and shelter. . . roof and raiment.
> What else?
> A chance!
> The best chance we can give to begin and to become.
> A chance to get past rock and reef into the channel and
> direction and control to survive the current.
>
> What children need is a set of carefully crafted,
> somewhat magical touchstones
> which, in youth, transform into moorings,
> giving first the security of place
> and then giving growing vessels
> a chance to be built strong in still water.

Later the touchstones transform again–
into paddle, rudder, and stern,
allowing fresh, new pilots to negotiate and navigate
the incredible currents of adult life.

The magic touchstones that children need,
and that parents owe,
are values–
values that hold us, secure us, guide us."

Teaching your children values is an integral part of parenting. The wisdom of Mr. Dale Anderson reinforces this responsibility.

❖

Mr. Russ Gibb

"The coming together and sharing in a classroom discussion is a repast that lasts a lifetime."

It doesn't take long for a teacher to learn that if you listen carefully to your students, you will soon be carefully taught.

After 35 years as a high school teacher, I have learned several important life lessons from my students.

First, never turn your back on your students. Think about it. The obvious meaning. The blackboard scene, chalk and spit balls flying. Yet, the deeper meaning is that students are young and developing personalities and have to know that someone will always listen and understand the trials and tribulations they are going through at the moment. Being a good listener is both important to the teacher and those he would teach.

The second is never miss a meal. Mealtime is important, but the most important meal is the fulfillment of intellectual feeding and the communal of breaking bread. Intellectual discussions with one's younger charges are as satisfying and fulfilling as mom's Sunday dinner. The coming together and sharing in a classroom discussion is a repast that lasts a lifetime.

Third is when students get excited about learning, get out of their way. Over the years I have seen it happen. One student gets an idea, and before long, others are talking about it. It spreads like a prairie fire. Intellectual curiosity and the desire to learn

Mr. Russ Gibb, "Night Call," The Mutual Broadcasting Company tele-phone radio talk show, Detroit, Michigan, 1972.

grow, and at this point the teacher should be passive and let the students' curiosity and zest for learning take them where it may.

Yes, over the years I have learned many things from my students. They have taught me that immortality is not something carved in stone or on plaques placed upon walls, but that true immortality is when your shared ideas are engraved in the hearts and minds of your students.

The greatest lesson one can ever learn is to love and be loved in return.

Commentary:

> "The one exclusive sign of a thorough knowledge is the power of teaching."
>
> – Aristotle

❖

Mr. Roy Miller

"The insignificance of each member of society may seem obvious but I subscribe to the oft-quoted Einstein phrase, 'Astronomically speaking, man is insignificant yet he is the astronomer.'"

I grew up in the depth of the Great Depression on the edge of the destitute Appalachian plateau. During my childhood I was keenly aware of the safety and support of the extended family, especially under adverse conditions. As Germany completed the capture of Europe and drove England back across the English Channel, I eagerly joined the Army Air Corps.

Life in the military acquainted me with the necessity for extensive cooperation between large groups of unrelated individuals who served a common cause. As one member of a 10-man crew on a B-17 bomber over the Reich, I painfully realized how precious life is. The only chance for survival depended primarily upon luck, aided in a small way by the skill and cooperation of my fellow crew members.

Suffice it to say, WWII ended favorably for me and the GI Bill extended opportunities beyond my wildest dreams. I gloried at my privilege of being alive and was profoundly awed at the mystery behind the scheme of things. It appeared to me society was composed of groups of mankind acting much like individuals and unconsciously following a pattern like water running downhill.

Mr. Roy Miller, 1980

I realized I wanted to devote my remaining life to raising a family while performing work in which I might possibly contribute to society in a basic manner. I decided I should train to teach physical sciences at the beginning college level where the young adults are searching for a foothold among their fellows.

I met my future wife my first day in college and later, with her support and three children, accepted a teaching position at a junior college. Teaching has been a stable lifestyle and the remuneration sufficient to support a family with reasonable comfort. The children have all joined the professions upon completing college and have families of their own. My wife and I enjoy retirement immensely and the results of some 40 years in the classroom have allowed a life more grand that I ever dreamed possible.

To spend a working lifetime as a teacher with young adults, continually dealing with man's discoveries and current concepts of the physical universe, has been completely satisfying. My duties have allowed me to conduct a class each semester for the non-science major. A majority of these students were preparing to be elementary teachers and thirsty for knowledge of how progress in mathematics, physics, chemistry, geology, astronomy, etc. continues to open new avenues of approach to the mystery of our universe.

In studying this area of knowledge, a student invariable recognizes the contributions of great minds of the past and their relation to the societies in which they lived. It becomes apparent that individuals can progress in their search for meaning to their existence only through the support and resources of society as a whole. We live in a time when transportation, communication and machines have aided mental processes and have abruptly changed the controls civilization has developed for all living relationships on earth.

I believe each person should be encouraged to contemplate the mystery of the universe and develop a desire to further a search for some comprehension. I am satisfied that my choice of teaching has allowed me to give some stimulus to those searching. Individual contribution toward finding a place for man in the "Big Scheme" is a responsibility we all feel. As we shoulder the burden, society as a whole benefits. The insignificance of each member of society may seem obvious but I subscribe to the oft-quoted Einstein phrase, "Astronomically speaking, man is insignificant yet he is the astronomer."

Commentary:

The wisdom Mr. Roy Miller shares with us reflects his essence. Reading his philosophy expanded my universe.

There is great wisdom in all of the preceding philosophies. However, other extremely important observations occurred. First, the philosophy of life statements that my patients shared with me not only impacted my life but also provided a most meaningful experience for them.

Second, the process of seeking wisdom from people who are close to us, particularly older people, is not usually pursued in our daily lives. When we ask others to express their innermost thoughts, we not only acquire a greater wisdom, but we are able to make a more significant and gratifying connection.

"The contemplation of celestial things
will make a man both speak and think
more sublimely and magnificently when
he comes down to human affairs."

– Cicero

Mrs. Martha Rockefeller

"Be a good girl, be responsible, kind, love and develop
a good attitude."

When I made my appearance in the world on August 21, 1918, it was in the home in which I would live for nine years. It was also in this house, at age 9, that I talked to my dying mother. The day before her death she took my hand and said to me, "Be a good girl, be responsible, kind, love and develop a good attitude."

I didn't understand these words, so my mother wrote them down for me. They were like the word God. You can't feel or see, but you know they will help shape your life. She had underlined the words <u>responsible</u>, <u>love</u> and <u>good attitude</u>.

During Thanksgiving of 1926 my mother was preparing our dinner of traditional turkey, dressing, cranberry sauce and pumpkin pie when a neighbor lady stopped by. She was crying because she didn't have food for her family of five. My mother packed up the meal she had cooked, put it in our red cart and took it to this woman's home. For our dinner we had a two-quart jar of chicken which my mother had canned.

A similar incident was repeated 28 years later when my daughter, Pat, came home and was crying because a very dear friend of hers wasn't having Thanksgiving because both parents weren't working. They had no electricity and no food. After a

Mrs. Martha Rockefeller, 1998

big discussion, we decided we would have our Thanksgiving later. My daughter went to the garage, got her red wagon down from where it was stored, and used it to take the meal to her friend's house.

When I see a red wagon today, I picture Thanksgiving being taken to someone less fortunate. I have lived as my mother asked me to, and I can say that after all these years I know what those words mean. I still have them.

Commentary:

The words of Mrs. Martha Rockefeller and of the other patients who have shared their philosophies of life will always be remembered. They will continually serve to guide me as the written words of Mrs. Rockefeller's mother have assisted in directing her life. Mrs. Rockefeller still possesses these words and I will always keep the written words of my patients. The importance of writing one's wisdom for another is emphasized in her philosophy of life statement.

In the book *Days of Grace*, the author Arthur Ashe ends his memoir with a letter to his daughter. I am confident that his intention was to record his wisdom for his daughter so that it would always remain with her. In the last section of this correspondence, he writes:

> "I end, Camera, as I began, with family. In nearly every civilization of which I have heard, the family is the central social unit, the base and foundation of the culture. You are a member of the eleventh identifiable generation of a family on my side and the fourth generation on your mother's side. We tried to prepare you as best we can to lead as happy and productive a life as possible. Along the way you will stumble, and perhaps even fall; but that, too, is normal and to be expected. Get up, get back on your feet, chastened but wiser, and continue on down the road.
>
> "I may not be walking with you all the way, or even much of the way, as I walk with you now. Don't be angry with me if I am not there in person, alive and well, when you need me. I would like nothing more than to be with you always. Do not feel sorry for me if I am gone. When we were together, I loved you deeply and you gave me so much happiness I can never repay you. Camera, wherever I am when you feel sick at heart and weary of life, or when you stumble and fall and don't know if you can get up again, think of me. I will be watching and smiling and cheering you on."

❖

A Tribute to My Mentor
John L. Ulrich, M.D.

Dr. John L. Ulrich, who was a most distinguished physician and a remarkable human being, is the inspiration for this book. As I mentioned in the introduction, I wish that I had asked Dr. Ulrich to put his philosophy of life in writing. This feeling eventually prompted me to ask several of my patients for their personal philosophies.

A patient, Mr. Robert Dougherty, echoes my sentiments when he writes, "As I've journeyed through life, I have met many famous people both in and out of the sporting world. But the one person who left a lasting impression on me was Dr. John Ulrich. From our very first meeting, I realized I was in a room with a very special person—one devoted to his family and to his God. He deeply cared for his patients, and especially me, as he always asked how my wife and children were doing. His last words to me at every visit were 'May God bless you and your family.'"

Because I do not have Dr. Ulrich's recorded philosophy, I am including a letter he wrote to Marcy and me which offers a glimpse of the essence of this extraordinary person.

John L. Ulrich, M.D.
(1915-1997)

JOHN L. ULRICH, M.D.

12-16-92

Dear Tom and Marcy —

Thank you so much for
your remembrances of
Christmas : the peas and
poinsettias have helped with
the "cheer" —; we will treasure
your kindness.

I am positive your precious
children are looking forward
to sharing your Florida
trip. Our hearts warm each
time their names are mentioned.
Please hug them for us.

We know the time of R&R
will be so good for you
both. Enjoy the pleasant
respites, life affords you,
while you can.

May almighty God touch
each of you with His
blessings of the spirit
as you travel and
stretch your souls.

Love John & Marlie

Reflections

To finish the moment, to find the journey's
end in every step of the road, to live the
greatest number of good hours, is wisdom.

– Ralph Waldo Emerson

Listen to the Whispers

To Marcy With Love

You are the reason
You are my rainbow
You are a dream
Each moment is precious.

The kindness from others sustains me
The wisdom from others guides me
The thought of you uplifts me
Each moment is precious.

Listen to the whispers
They are sent from above
Listen to the whispers
The greatest of these is love.

When you are tired and weary,
Rest your head on my shoulder.
Lift your eyes to the heavens above
The greatest of these is love.

"Life is struggle, embrace it.
Life is beauty, praise it.
Life is sorrow, experience it.
Life has a purpose, fulfill it."

Listen to the whispers
They are sent from above
Listen to the whispers
The greatest of these is love.

Look back to learn
Look forward with you
Listen to the whispers
Listen to the whispers.

There is wisdom in your life
Remember
There are special people in your life
Remember.

My heart is yours forever
You are with me always
This is from above
The greatest of these is love.

Listen to the whispers
Listen to the whispers
They are from above
The greatest of these is love.

T.P.W.

A Gentle Breeze

A Tribute to Bette and Don Mys

The sound of your voice
The sparkle in your eyes
The bloom of a magnolia
The leaves on the trees.

The morning sun
    in all its splendor
The snow-capped mountains
    in their grandeur
A field of flowers
The leaves on the trees
A gentle breeze.

Search for the essence
Two souls meet
Peace, purity, faith
A friendship forever.

Close your eyes
Silent words are heard
The stars grace the sky
A field of flowers
A friendship forever.

T.P.W.

Fly Forever

To my friends and patients who have lost a loved one

Butterfly in the sun
Spread your wings
Fly forever
Fly for those
No longer here
Fly forever.

Rushing river
Silent stream
Calm the souls
Of those
Who remain
Who remain.

Pray for peace
The strength to bear
Pray for courage
The will to care.

Butterfly in the sun
Spread your wings
Fly forever
Fly for those
No longer here
Fly forever.

Lay aside every weight
Run the race
That is set before us
With humility and grace.

Rushing river
Silent stream
Calm the souls
Of those
Who remain
Who remain.

Butterfly in the sun
Rushing river
Silent stream
Bless the child
Who remains
Bless the child
Bless the child
Fly forever
Fly forever.

T.P.W.

$$\mathscr{E}pilogue$$

Mr. and Mrs. John Santarelli were originally my patients and have now become wonderful friends. I met both of them in the early years of my practice. Mr. Santarelli's hobby is wood-carving. Mrs. Santarelli's hobby is handicrafts. Mr. Santarelli handcarved a beautiful duck and two wooden boots for me. I treasure their gifts but I treasure their friendship more.

Johnnie and Marie Santarelli once shared this story with me about their nephew, Mr. Earl St. John, who lived in northern Michigan. He was occupied primarily cutting firewood and hauling lumber. Times were extremely difficult economically, but he always maintained a positive spirit. Earl's wife suggested that in order to increase and diversify their business, he should write the name "Forest Products" on his truck. Earl followed his wife's advice and the name "Forest Products" appeared on his truck shortly thereafter.

Their business prospered and the name Forest Products became well known. This was a factor in a large corporation having an interest in Mr. St. John's business. Mr. St. John went on to pioneer the mechanization of logging and Forest Products became one of the largest logging contractors in the nation. Many years later, Mr. St. John served as a director of the Federal

Handcrafted by Mr. John Santarelli, Dearborn Heights, Michigan, July 1992

Reserve Board, Region Nine, in Minneapolis, Minnesota–a long way from cutting firewood and hauling lumber.

I remember when Johnnie and Marie were sitting in my office telling me this story. I thought at that time that I had to share this success story with my children so that they would realize that any dream or aspiration is possible. Earl's story reinforced my belief that each of us can achieve whatever we dream or hope for in life. Anything is possible if we set our mind to it and believe in it. This belief helped me to pursue writing this book. So the next time you are having Sunday dinner with your family, perhaps on a wooden table, remember Johnnie and Marie's story about their beloved nephew and share it with your children so that they will learn to believe in themselves and persevere in their endeavors.

There is another important message from this story that has greater meaning to me. There are thoughts or actions each day that may seem trivial but, in fact, have great significance. In the case of Johnnie and Marie's nephew, it meant the creation of a new business and economic stability. In our daily lives, this can be a positive word to another, a smile, a handshake, or the seeking of wisdom from people who will help you in your life. As physicians, we must never forget this. At every encounter with a patient, the smallest positive gesture can have great impact. This can be extended to all facets of our lives.

In the Introduction, I mentioned two defining moments in my life. This book is my third defining moment. The wisdom from my patients has reinforced my philosophy to find the correct way to live, seek virtue, and always be kind to others. It is important to me to make this effort on a daily basis. I have learned more about myself by seeking the wisdom of life through my patients. My patients' wisdom has given me a greater clarity in my life and a stronger foundation for the correct way to live. I now have a greater inner peace because of this. Adversity is easier to deal with. This process is life-transforming for every person who undertakes this search. As a physician, medicine becomes more satisfying and patients become more interesting. The interaction can be comforting for the patient as well as for the doctor. Each can learn wisdom from the other.

The observation that the wisdom of a person and the spiritual essence of a person are intertwined, meshed and can merge with each other was discussed in the Introduction. I believe that this connection is significant. More importantly, it gives each of us a different avenue to learn about the other. When you seek one, you will find the other. The wisdom of a person will be life-transforming; the connection with his or her spiritual essence will be life-comforting.

Mr. Gilbert Ropes celebrated his 88th birthday this year. He has been a patient for 14 years. His philosophy of life has great meaning to all of us.

> "In everything I do, I strive for perfection.
> But, I do not expect to achieve it.
>
> Therefore, if I do the best I can with the talents
> I have and bring a little happiness to others,
> Then I am satisfied and also happy."

His statement parallels the spiritual essence and wisdom found in Hebrews 12:1:

> . . .since we are surrounded by so great a
> cloud of witnesses, let us lay aside every
> weight, and the sin which so easily ensnares
> us, and let us run with endurance the race that
> is set before us.

It is my sincere hope that each of you will try to seek wisdom and make a connection with those who are important to you. This is one way to help you find yourself, have greater content-ment in life, and accomplish great things. This search does not replace the importance of your religious beliefs or values; rather, it helps you become more aware of them and their significance in your life. There is great simplicity in this endeavor. It is avail-able to us each day. We are enriched in the process. We develop stronger and more fulfilling friendships. We change as people and become better physicians to our patients. I hope the philosophy of life statements from my patients not only add wisdom to your life but encourage you to pursue the search for wisdom from people who are important to you in your life.

The pursuit of wisdom makes each day more meaningful and enjoyable, for as Walt Whitman wrote, "Some people are so much sunshine to the square inch."

About the Author

Thomas P. Waldinger, M.D., is a board certified dermatologist in private practice in Dearborn, Michigan. He specializes in geriatric dermatology and skin cancer. His wife, Marcy, is the Administrative Director of the University of Michigan Comprehensive Cancer Center. They are the proud parents of a son, Jason, and a daughter, Emily. The Waldinger family resides in Ann Arbor, Michigan.

Dr. Waldinger received a Bachelor of Science Degree with High Distinction from the University of Michigan in 1976. He graduated from the University of Michigan Medical School in 1980. His post-graduate training was also completed at the University of Michigan in the Department of Family Practice and the Department of Dermatology from July 1980 through June 1985. Dr. Waldinger served as an emergency staff physician at Outer Drive Hospital, Allen Park, Michigan, from July 1981 through June 1982. Since 1985, he has been on staff at Oakwood Hospital in Dearborn, Michigan.

Dr. Waldinger is the author or co-author of 11 peer-reviewed publications in the field of dermatology. His honors include graduating Phi Beta Kappa from the University of Michigan in 1976 and being named a Paul Harris Fellow, Dearborn Rotary Club, in 1986. Dr. Waldinger was also included in *The Best Doctors in America-Midwest® Region, 1996-1997*, Woodward and White, Inc., and in *The Best Doctors in America® Fourth Listing, 1998-1999*, Woodward and White, Inc.